## I Have Looked Death In The Face

Biography of
William Porcher DuBose

A book about a man who had a real impact on our church in his day. His making christianity a _personal_ thing impacts us still.

JH Wibo
Feb, '97

## BOOKS BY JOHN M. WILSON

*Oh, Yes, I Want To Go Home*
(Historical Novel set in the
American
War Between The States)

*Final Furlough*
(Short Stories about the
American
War Between The States
and other Subjects of Interest)

*I Have Looked Death In The Face*
(Civil War Biography of
William Porcher DuBose of
South Carolina.
Soldier, Philosopher,
Theologian)

# I HAVE LOOKED DEATH IN THE FACE

Biography of William Porcher DuBose,
Soldier, Philosopher, Theologian

By: John M. Wilson

Published By:
Paint Rock Publishing, Inc
Kingston, Tennessee

1996

Requests for permission to make copies
of any part of the work should be mailed to:
Permissions
Paint Rock Publishing, Inc.
118 Dupont Smith Lane
Kingston, Tennessee 37763
(423) 376-3892


**Publisher's Cataloging in Publication**


Wilson, John Morris, 1939-
    "I Have Looked Death In The Face" ; biography of William
Porcher DuBose, Soldier, Philosopher and Theologian/ by
John M. Wilson
        p. cm.
        Includes bibliographical references
        ISBN 0-9649394-2-8

        1. United States — Civil War, 1861-1865—History—Episcopal
Church—Biography. I. Title.

PS357315766    1996                          813'.54
                                             QB196-200


Manufactured in the United States of America
First Edition

This Book is dedicated to the memories of
Professor Charles W. Wilson, Jr.
and Barbara Bookman Wilson,
who gave me their passion for history

# CONTENTS

## BACKGROUND MATERIAL

## PLATES

## FIGURES

## TABLES

## ACKNOWLEDGEMENTS

I would like to thank my wife, Faye, for patience shown during the time and travels taken to write this book. She encouraged and aided in the research from the very beginning. Father Stephen Freeman of St. Stephen's Episcopal Church in Oak Ridge, Tennessee, gave me encouragement during the writing. My brother, C.W. Wilson, III, and my sister, Catherine Anne Wilson, read the manuscript and improved it substantially. My son, history teacher Jack Wilson, reviewed the document and made excellent suggestions. Mr. Fred Troise made comments that improved the manuscript. I thank Reverends Jerry Stadel, Joe Diaz, Arthur Lee, John Cain, and Michael Davis of the Episcopal Diocese of South Florida for reinstalling in me the idea that research, thinking, and writing can be fun, if sometimes painful.

Many persons with libraries and historical associations provided assistance during research. Among these were Ms. Anne Armour of The University of the South; Vergiant Brown, Neuse Regional Public Library, Kinston, North Carolina; the staff of the South Carolina State Library and the Department of History and Archives in Columbia; and Ms. Jane Yates of the staff of the Library and Archives at The Citadel, Charleston, South Carolina.

The people in the libraries in Columbia and Charleston were quick to correct me on two points for which I will remain grateful: William DuBose's middle name is pronounced **Por shay'**, not **Porch' er**. The French Huguenot influence lives on! The conflict in which DuBose served was not the Civil War but the "**War Between the States.**" At times, it was also known as the "**Second American Revolution,**" "**The War of Northern Aggression,**" or, "**The War for Southern Independence.**"

Mr. Ric A. Wilson designed the cover and completed the book layout. His assistance and talent are gratefully acknowledged. The review and edit was done by Ms. Elizabeth Nash who assisted in improving the final quality of the document substantially. However, any errors are those of the writer alone. Lastly, thanks to Mrs. Judy Nelson, whose typing and formatting of this work produced a presentable, readable document. Final read-through was done by Ms. Phyllis Garman.

A final word about the format of this book: primary sources of information about DuBose and the military units he served are used wherever available. A house fire in the first decade of this century tragically destroyed many documents and probably photographs as well, so that DuBose personal primary sources are limited. In many places in this book, I have relied on secondary sources to provide additional information on conflicts, causes, reasons, history, etc. Because Mr. Webster defines *background*, as "Underlying or supporting causes, events, or settings," I have placed much of the secondary source information and explanations in boxes separate from the main text. You may overlook those details and read only the story of DuBose in the regular text, or, you can read the text and the *BACKGROUND* sections together to obtain a more complete picture of the larger events that dictated DuBose's early life.

*I Have Looked Death In The Face*

**Biography of
William Porcher DuBose**

# Chapter I

"The sage of Sewanee, revered by every generation
that came under his influence."
— A Sewanee student, later a Bishop

# INTRODUCTION

Portrait of W.P. DuBose near Retirement (circa 1910)
Courtesy, The University of the South Archives

# INTRODUCTION

# CHAPTER I

## INTRODUCTION

In December of 1862 two influential South Carolinians made a wartime decision that would ultimately impact millions of Americans as yet unborn. One of the men was a general in the Army of the Confederate States of America. One was a bishop in the Episcopal Church of South Carolina. General Kershaw and Bishop Davis, with the help of others, removed a young Confederate line officer, William Porcher DuBose, from a direct role on the battle line. They had in mind for him a position where his odds of surviving the Civil War were somewhat better. They wanted him to be a chaplain.

They made the decision because by this time, DuBose had participated in three battles and numerous skirmishes, suffered three wounds, been taken captive, and held as a prisoner of war all within six-months. Bishop Davis hurriedly ordained DuBose as a deacon in the Episcopal Church and Kershaw requested him as chaplain-at-large to his brigade. As a result of this decision, DuBose did indeed survive the war. He also became one of the more important theologians in the history of the Episcopal Church and one of her most influential and revered teachers. Millions of people have benefited from DuBose's unique personalization of Christianity presented through his voluminous writings.

The Reverend Moultrie Guerry in *Men Who Made Sewanee* tells a story of the elderly Dr. DuBose when he met Miss Helen Keller at a reception. It is a story that clearly illustrates his magnetism and charisma. The blind hostess had shaken many hands, but when she felt Dr. DuBose's hand, she impulsively ran her fingers lightly over his small straight stature and face. Through her fingers she seemed to see his face, and indeed his very soul. She drew him quickly to her and kissed him as though she had discovered her own father.[1]

William Porcher DuBose was born in 1836 in rural South Carolina where he was raised and schooled on a slave-holding plantation. As was desirable for the times, he received a military collegiate education and graduated from The Citadel as ranking officer and first in his class. Page 59 of this book shows DuBose in Confederate military dress. Staff of The Citadel Library and Archives identified the jacket as a Citadel military uniform that DuBose modified for use in the Holcombe Legion by adding his rank and unit insignia, apparently a common Confederate practice.

While in The Citadel, DuBose experienced a religious conversion. He went on to the University of Virginia in Charlottesville where he received multiple Masters of Arts degrees, principally in romance languages and moral science. He followed his religious calling and next entered the Episcopal seminary. He was able to complete one and one-half years in the seminary before the Civil War interrupted this phase of his life.

DuBose entered the service and was assigned to the defense of South Carolina with the Holcombe Legion, which was later converted by Governor Pickens to the service of the Confederacy. Clearly, DuBose did not have a good 1862. During that year he was wounded twice at the Second Battle of Manassas, captured at the Battle of South Mountain (Boonsboro Gap), and held several weeks in Fort Delaware Federal Prisoner of War Camp. He was paroled and then seriously wounded during the Battle of Kinston, North Carolina. Influential friends realized that DuBose would never survive the war at this rate, so they arranged a position as chaplain with Major

General Joseph Kershaw's Brigade. DuBose was ordained by Bishop Davis as a deacon in the Episcopal Church and served in Kershaw's Brigade until the close of hostilities in 1865.

DuBose returned from the war to the physical and mental devastation that South Carolina had become. He was ordained as a priest in the newly reunited Episcopal Church of the United States. He served as rector in several war-destroyed parishes, narrowly "escaped" election as Bishop of South Carolina, and then became chaplain of The University of the South in Sewanee, Tennessee. During his long career there he served terms as Dean of the new School of Theology and Professor of Theology and other subjects until his death in 1918.

Dr. DuBose wrote books on the New Testament, St. Paul, and Episcopal theology which became widely circulated. He is regarded by many prominent churchmen as one of the more important theologians produced by the Episcopal Church in the United States. During his lifetime he received honorary degrees of Doctor of Sacred Theology by Columbia University, Doctor of Divinity from the General Theological Seminary in New York, and Doctor of Civil Laws from The University of the South.

The title of this book, *I Have Looked Death in the Face,* was chosen because of its applicability to William Porcher DuBose's wartime experiences–both as a thrice-wounded soldier and as a chaplain who saw the obvious approach of death in the faces of numerous soldiers. The phrase is from DuBose's final words to his family and friends as he, at the age of eighty-three, was gracefully leaving this earth. His last words were reported by Bishop Bratton and the entire quotation from which the title was chosen was, "You need not think that I have not been thinking of death. I have been looking at it from all sides. I have looked death in the face, and felt it in my body, and I am ready to face it. If God should take me tonight I would be glad. The Eternal Father, the risen Christ, the Blessed Holy Ghost have been my companions."[2]

Why a book about William DuBose? I have asked myself this question many times during my research and writing. Articles as well as a few books have been written about DuBose and his thoughts. Why *this* book? I pursued this project mainly because I am intrigued by the transition that must have occurred within the beliefs and faith of a man who was born into an elite, slave-holding family, served as a soldier and a chaplain in the bloodiest war ever fought on American soil, and finally became a loved and respected theologian. I have collected all materials possible on DuBose's war experiences in an attempt to follow the transition of a man from privileged gentleman, to warrior, to chaplain, to theologian and teacher.

I also wanted to write this book because I am intrigued by the Civil War. I believe that I had no choice but to be a Civil War buff because I was raised on the site of Redoubt Number One of the Battle of Nashville (December 1864). It was one of the last major battles of the Civil War and most probably the battle that sounded the deathknell for the Confederacy. Redoubt Number One was the strong point for General John Bell Hood's depleted Southern Army and the last to fall. Hood's soldiers knew, as they dug in on their blizzard-swept hillside that December night, what crushing blows would come the next day from the vastly superior Federal force. Our yard was covered with breastworks and foxholes deep and sturdy enough to be still quite obvious eighty years later. While children, my brother, sister and I found and cherished Minie balls, grapeshot, pieces of cannonballs, bayonets, and other flotsam of war miraculously preserved after nearly a century of lying in the shallow soils of the Redoubt.

**The Minie Ball**

A Minie Ball is a patented invention of a Frenchman, Captain M. Minie. He designed a new bullet that "made the rifle practical for war." The bullet was designed for rifled or grooved barrels as had been other bullets, but the Minie was unique, because it was conical and therefore more accurate, yet it could fire from a dirty barrel and still completely fill the barrel so that the gasses could not escape past the bullet. The Minie Ball was the standard bullet for both armies in the Civil War and is probably the most common artifact found at the scenes of battles or skirmishes.

We had many spirited arguments as to whether particular bullets were of the Yankee or Rebel variety. These discussions and arguments encompassed other aspects of Civil War history because my mother was born and bred of a Cincinnati Yankee family. The only way I could justify to myself that I was a total Southerner was to rationalize that every time I fell as a child and cut a knee and bled, it was "the Yankee blood" coming out. By the time I was ten or twelve years old, I had no Yankee left in me. I thus became a pure Southerner, at least in my mind.

Perhaps this is an appropriate place to make a confession. We were told while growing up that my Yankee mother was related to William Tecumseh Sherman, the scourge of the South. Upon conducting some genealogical research, we did indeed find (to our horror) that Sherman was apparently my Mother's great uncle, related by marriage. We Southerners do have our crosses to bear. Sherman also had two step-brothers who were generals in the Union Army. Two additional relatives of mine from the Columbus, Ohio, area fought in the war—one for the Union and one for the South.

However, on the other side of the family, one of my paternal great-grandfathers, John Wesley Morris (after whom I was named) served honorably in the Confederate Army with a Kentucky unit, the Seventh Kentucky Mounted Infantry Volunteers, along with his brother, Moses Franklin Morris. Moses Morris died of a "congestive chill" in 1864 while returning to his unit after a furlough. My other paternal great-grandfather, Silas Charles Wilson, also served four years in the Confederate Army. We have identified a total of twenty-three relatives from western Kentucky who fought in the Civil War, 22 for the Confederacy and one for the North.

I also remember that most of our family vacations while I was growing up included visits to the important battlefields of the Civil War. I was raised on talk of Manassas (Bull Run), Gettysburg, Shiloh, Antietam, the Wilderness, Atlanta, Petersburg, Fort Donelson, Fort Pillow, Fredricksburg, Chancelorsville, Murfreesboro, and Franklin. I thrilled and shivered to hear accounts of such events as the ill-fated charge of Pickett's brigade up Cemetery Ridge at Gettysburg where the bullets were flying so thick that many would strike together in mid-air, actually fusing and falling to the ground as one.

My life and Civil War interests intersected with the life of William Porcher DuBose in the early 1990's while I was undergoing training to become a Perpetual Deacon in the Episcopal Church. I read a statement by Urban T. Holmes that "There is no evidence that he (DuBose) or his family held anything but the prevailing socio-political viewpoint of their class in South Carolina at the time of the Civil War."[3] I reasoned that Holmes was saying that William Porcher DuBose was definitely a secessionist and an "unreconstructed Southerner." Many of his family, friends, and schoolmates were killed during the war. Both of his parents died during the long, bitter conflict. DuBose was very much a product of the times as he read accounts of the imminent war in the South Carolina newspapers. He no doubt believed as his neighbors did, that states' rights and protection of one's homeland were first and foremost.

How good a soldier was DuBose? Considering his frail constitution, quite good. The numerous citations made in official battle reports about his courage in virtually every conflict in which he fought are quite impressive. As examples, official records following the Battle of South Mountain had this to say about DuBose: "Colonel Stevens especially commended the conduct of Colonel McMaster, Major Hilton, Captain Durham and Adjt. W.P. DuBose. The latter officer was captured after night while endeavoring with a small force to reconnoiter the enemy's front."[4]

Following the same battle, his commanding officer, Colonel Stevens lamented that, ". . . in him I have lost my right arm, and the service as noble, as pure-minded, as fearless an officer as ever battled for his country."[4] And following the Battle for the Bridges of Kinston, the records noted, "especially the gallant conduct of Adju. W.P. DuBose . . . "[4]

How good a theologian was DuBose? According to preeminent theologians from the time after his teaching and writing, he is perhaps the most important in the history of the American Episcopal Church. He retained his freshness and youthful thought to an age far beyond most of us: his *The Reason of Life*[5] and *Turning Points in My Life*[6] were written at ages seventy-six and seventy-seven, respectively.

How good a teacher was DuBose? The best, according to most of his former students, among whom were bishops and church leaders. Several have commented that DuBose was the single most important force in their lives. His students left The University of the South with a deep love and respect for Dr. DuBose. One student who eventually became a bishop said, "He represented the spirit of The University of the South. To the students he became the sage of Sewanee, revered by every generation that came under his influence."

This book, then, is an inquiry into William Porcher DuBose's life, particularly in the years just before and during his long and successful tenure at The University of the South, a period largely defined by the Civil War and its aftermath. I feel more confident when researching and writing about the history of the Civil War than I do about the complex thoughts and writings of such a well-respected theologian as DuBose. I use quotes from DuBose's writings when they help explain an answer, and I also present a brief synopsis of his theology. But, I will leave the detailed theological inquiries to those so inclined and so trained.

# Chapter II

"Dubose was a product of a now-vanished society."
— Bishop Stephen F. Bayne

## FAMILY BACKGROUND AND EARLY LIFE
### (1836-1861)

Plantation that survived Sherman's March, on the Ashley River
LC

# CHAPTER II

## FAMILY BACKGROUND AND EARLY LIFE

William Porcher DuBose was the son of an old, aristocratic South Carolina family. His heritage was French Huguenot, but his ancestors became Anglicans early. In 1686 Isaac DuBose arrived in South Carolina with emigrants from France and Switzerland and they settled along the Santee and Cooper Rivers. According to William DuBose, that colony still retained its French nature at the time of the writing of his *Reminiscences* (circa 1911).[7] His pride in his Huguenot heritage is obvious in his writings.

### French Huguenot Influence in South Carolina

Most of the French Huguenots who remained in the South Carolina "Low Country" were converted and absorbed into the Church of England, and the community around St. John's Episcopal Church was immersed in the English Anglican Church. Church services were attended by all, though generally the men did not receive communion or participate actively in church affairs. After the Revolutionary War the church underwent drastic changes because of its close pre-Revolutionary war ties with England and its subsequent loss of bishops (they all returned to England). This situation was a real problem until three American presbyters were consecrated as bishops in the Church (thanks to the Scottish Church in the case of the first new bishop.) The American Episcopal Church thus became self-sustaining.

Three generations after the first Isaac, the DuBose family married into the Sinkler family, one of the richer families in the area. The Santee River bottom soil was as productive as the Mississippi River bottom lands in the southwestern and southern United States and successful farming added to the family wealth. The family was active during the American Revolution. William DuBose's grandfather, Samuel DuBose, was born just after the American Revolution. William's father was educated in the North at Yale University then returned to inherit and purchase extensive property, including one plantation on the Cooper River and others in middle St. John's County.

William Porcher DuBose was born in Winnsboro, South Carolina, on April 11, 1836, and baptized soon after birth by the Reverend Mr. Shand, Rector of St. Johns Parish. For health reasons DuBose's father, Theodore Samuel Marion DuBose, purchased Farmington Plantation, which consisted of three thousand acres and was located nine miles north of Winnsboro. Moving from the immediate vicinity of the true coastal plain with its accompanying excessive heat, humidity, and mosquitoes had become a necessity for the health of Theodore DuBose. William DuBose was born next door to the inn that had served as Lord Cornwallis' headquarters during the American Revolution. Eighty-eight years after Cornwallis' occupation, General William T. Sherman used the same inn as his headquarters during his devastating march through South Carolina and Georgia.

According to DuBose, in his youth he had only occasional "religious moments," but he was brought up under the religious influence of his mother and his Aunt Betsy. According to DuBose, Aunt Betsy was " . . . the most beautiful, and immediately influential religious character, I have ever come in contact with. My mother had always kept us close to the church and its instructions, but she was not so aggressively pious as my Aunt Betsy." Almost single-handedly, Aunt Betsy converted the men in the area to communicants and persuaded them to take a more active part in the church.[7]

In speaking of DuBose's early life, Bishop Stephen F. Bayne remarked that, "DuBose was the product of a now-vanished society; and the virtues and graces bred in him were deeply formed by that society. The world of his youth was the world of plantation life– opulent of its kind, easy, filled with cousins and friends."[8]

DuBose said that he was " . . . related to everybody in St. Johns. The whole Low-Country was a paradise for boys. We lived on horseback and visited indiscriminately all the plantations, dropping in sometimes ten at a time, horses and all."[7] DuBose's formative years were spent in the plantation ideal– a plantation that was home to a patriarchal family, an agricultural and mechanical community and a school. The community made the farm and house tools and clothing and grew most of its food.

DuBose learned to read when he began Mrs. Atkinson's school as an eight-year-old. He recalled his delight in discovering the *Arabian Nights*: "One day, rummaging up in a closet in the boy's room (we had large rooms upstairs, one a boys' room, one a girls', etc.), I came across an unabridged large copy of the *Arabian Nights*. After that I was lost for an indefinite time. I had a passion of lying flat on my stomach and reading. Accidentally or purposely, folk coming along stepped on me, etc., but I never knew. I only crawled a little farther, until at last I moved up under the table."[7] (Writer's note: I can truly relate to this story. An avid reader as a boy, I could, like DuBose, totally immerse myself in a book; the house could have burned down around me and I would scarcely have noticed it.)

At the end of the first year of school, William DuBose took first place in scholarship and won a copy of G & F's First Reader as his prize. After Mrs. Atkinson's School he attended a school run by Mr. J.W. Hudson in Winnsboro. DuBose was a pet pupil of Hudson's and did well in all subjects, except for mathematics. DuBose became proficient in Latin, but both his teachers and his father failed in their efforts to teach him mathematics. His father decided to send DuBose

to The Citadel, with its emphasis on engineering and related mathematics, where he hoped his son would solve this problem.
Scholarship and education were clearly first priorities with Samuel
DuBose; besides, a gentleman in the plantation business must have
skills in mathematics to be successful. For the one year before
DuBose went to The Citadel, he was tutored in mathematics for several hours every day.

Even if he had had no problem with mathematics, it would still
have been appropriate for DuBose to continue his education at The
Citadel, because a military education was considered most necessary
and desirable for a Southern gentleman.

In *Reminiscences,* DuBose recounts the way his father dealt with
the math problem:

> He undertook to teach me himself, but he made a worse
> failure than Mr. Hudson. His hopes were on me and he
> had determined that each of his sons should have a good
> education, including college and university, and after that
> a professional training, though all our family had for two
> hundred years been planters. He did a most *heroic* thing.
> Instead of letting me go to college where I could have
> entered and for which I was prepared, my father decided
> to send me to a military school, The Citadel, for which I
> was physically unprepared, and mentally also, owing to
> my trouble with mathematics. One year before I went to
> The Citadel, Wyatt Aiken came to Mr. Hudson's to teach
> Mathematics. I have a distinct recollection of the day I
> went to him. Mind you, I was to begin Algebra and I
> knew not one word of Arithmetic. He said, 'We are start-
> ing now, and I want you to start right. Do this yourself.
> Ask no help, except from me.' That appealed to me, and
> turning my back on other things I set out to learn that lit-
> tle book. At home at night I puzzled over it and during
> the two hours at mid-day, and by the end of the year I had
> done it and done it myself. I didn't know what a revolu-
> tion I had worked in myself.[7]

William DuBose went to The Citadel in January 1852 (Plate 2). The large student body of one hundred students was divided into two groups: DuBose and the other incoming students were sent to the Arsenal Military Academy in Columbia, South Carolina, and the upperclassmen attended The Citadel in Charleston. DuBose applied himself and finished the first year as number one in his class and even number one in mathematics. In a proud moment, he was appointed as corporal in the corps of cadets.

In 1852 yellow fever swept Charleston. According to Thomas, most Cadets at The Citadel left their posts and went home without being properly furloughed. Believing those who left had listened to the unwise counsel of their fellow students rather than to the authorities, the Cadet Disciplinary Board later allowed these cadets to return to the Academy. This was instead of charging them with "willful abandonment of duty:" the Board did rebuke the cadets for taking safety over duty. DuBose and eight other cadets remained throughout the sickness panic. The Board said that all demerits against the nine were to be removed " . . . in consideration of the high estimate the Board put upon their conduct for remaining at their post until furlough."[7]

DuBose continued to do well the next year and was promoted to Sergeant of Cadets. During the beginning of the third year, the corps of cadets spent the summer in an expeditionary march through the upper counties of South Carolina. DuBose had many good memories of that summer through which the corps marched thirty miles every day. At times they moved so fast that they even became separated from their provisionary wagon.

About this time DuBose had an experience that he would remember clearly years later. After two years at The Citadel, during which he had excelled in every phase of scholarship at the school, he appeared to lose interest. He became careless and indifferent in his classes and wrote home to his mother in a homesick way. DuBose's father wrote him a strong letter, which DuBose would recall sixty years later. His father discussed the weakness, the folly, and the unmanliness of homesickness. The letter woke him up, and he persevered for the rest of the year. According to DuBose, it was too late, as he finished "only second" in his class after the end of the third year.

DuBose remembered that while at The Citadel during these years he lost some of his religious fervor and neglected his prayers. However, he thought that his temper and character seemed to have assigned him to the ministry from birth. He probably suspected that he would eventually enter the ministry.

In 1854 when he was going back to The Citadel for his fourth and final year, William DuBose underwent what he considered a profound religious "conversion experience." The experience was not that of a dramatic right-about-face or a Damascus Road scene: DuBose was not Saul of Tarsus. He was not changed in an instant from one path to another and his attraction to the ministry would likely have persisted regardless. Bishop Bayne speculates that DuBose probably would have still become the sturdy, conventional, thoughtful churchman to which his temperament and the life of his family and society predisposed him.[8] Nonetheless, DuBose considered the experience important enough for him to spend a year trying to sort out his thoughts and priorities.

During this return trip in 1854 DuBose and his two cousins, Dick Dwight and William Gaillard, accompanied DuBose's father to Columbia. Halfway to The Citadel they stopped for the night at a hotel where a famous actor was presenting a comedy in the little theater. After having what DuBose called "an uproarious time," the three boys retired to bed about midnight. The other two went to sleep, but DuBose said that a presence came into the room;

> It is a most singular thing—It was just as though a new world had opened to me, a new presence had come into my life and it was so absolute and positive, there was no mistaking it. I dreaded to go to sleep, lest it disappear. But

when I woke, it was there. When we took the cars the next morning I was still so afraid it might pass away that I left my friends and, sitting in the smoking car, thought it all over. Then I realized that it was a permanent change. When I got to The Citadel, I thought I ought to guard myself in its preservation, so I withdrew from my roommates, and that same older friend, Charles Haskell, with whom I had been on the march, being very anxious to have me room with him, we did room together. The rest of that year was spent in consolidating my gains. I was settling, fixing, and arranging myself. I corresponded with Stoney and we agreed to study together for the ministry.[7]

On November 19, 1854, DuBose was confirmed (a sacrament of recommitment practiced in the churches of the catholic community) by Bishop T.F. Davis at St. Michael's Church in Charleston. During the year he became Captain of the Corps, highest cadet officer in The Citadel, and he became an assistant professor in English and taught fourth-year English.

The following table is a reproduction of William P. DuBose's Citadel grades for the years 1852-1855 as obtained from the Archives of The Citadel.

| Course | 1852 | 1853 | 1854 | 1855 | 4-Year |
|---|---|---|---|---|---|
| Math | 1 | 1 | 2 | | 1.33 |
| French | 1 | 1 | | | 1.00 |
| Letters | 1 | | 2 | | 1.50 |
| Conduct | 14 | 12 | 8 | 6 | 10.00 |
| History | | 1 | | | 1.00 |
| Drawing | 7 | 2 | 10 | 6 | 7.00 |
| Nat Phil | | | 1 | | 1.00 |
| Astronomy | | | | 1 | 1.00 |
| Chemistry | | | | 1 | 1.00 |
| Engineering | | | | 2 | 2.00 |
| Mechanics | | | | 1 | 1.00 |
| Tactics | | | | 1 | 1.00 |
| Elocution | | | | 3 | 3.00 |
| Pol Sci | | | | 1 | 1.00 |
| **Average** | 4.80 | 4.00 | 4.60 | 2.44 | 3.96 |

TABLE 1. THE CITADEL ACADEMIC RECORD, W.P. DUBOSE

The conduct rankings are interesting. DuBose averaged only about tenth in his class in that category. While proving himself to be a model scholar, he apparently still managed to enjoy himself even though the professors did not always agree with the way in which he did so. Perhaps every wealthy plantation kid has a bit of trouble totally accepting other's authority. Or perhaps, having had slaves and body-servants all of his life, brass- and equipment- and shoe-polishing and uniform pressing did not appeal to him. Nonetheless, in December 1855 he graduated from The Citadel with first honors.

Following graduation, DuBose spent ten months with his extended family on the Low Country and Upper Country plantations in South Carolina. DuBose and his family were all from the Low Country of South Carolina. According to Mary Chesnut in her diary, there could be no question as to their loyalties during the war:

> The Up Country men were Union men generally, and the Low Country were seceders. The former growl; they never liked those aristocratic boroughs and parishes, they had themselves a good and prosperous country, a good constitution, and were satisfied. But they had to go–to leave all and fight for the others who brought on all the trouble, and who do not show much disposition to fight for themselves.[9]

DuBose and his relatives certainly fit in well with Mrs. Chesnut's analysis of the Low Country secessionists.

When DuBose returned home after graduation from The Citadel he began to experience health problems, particularly with his eyes. He contracted "granulated lids," a painful condition in which reading and even sleeping bring sharp discomfort every time the eyes blink or close. He also had a personal problem: he became "semi-committed" to a girl, though "they had never spoken of it." Even this tenuous attachment caused problems between DuBose and his father, who wanted William and his brothers to obtain as much education as possible and felt that too early a romantic attachment would prevent them from reaching that goal. Once again, education is a first priority for Southern gentlemen. Finally, DuBose explained these circumstances to the young lady's roommate, and the "semi-commitment" ended. Such a means at ending the relationship seems to lack gallantry, but apparently very little if any direct communication took place between the two young people. Could this have been a "lost first love" similar to Abraham Lincoln's? In his writings, DuBose never again mentions the young lady.

In October 1856 DuBose entered the University of Virginia at Charlottesville and registered in the Schools of Latin, Greek, French, and moral science. At that time a student could be a graduate in any number of schools. He was still having some trouble with his eyes, but by "careful and judicious use," they gradually improved.

In 1859 he received diplomas in Latin, French, and moral science. That year DuBose attended the Annual Diocesan Convention in Petersburg, Virginia, with his friend Thomas Dudley and his family. At that convention DuBose heard Bishop Johns preach and was impressed. He commented that "Bishop Johns was a very eloquent, earnest preacher–marvelously so!" DuBose returned to the University of Virginia the next session and earned diplomas in Greek, mathematics, and physics (natural philosophy). During the second year DuBose became involved with fraternity politics. This diversion once almost led to a duel with pistols between two of his fraternity brothers. DuBose was apparently not personally involved, but the incident obviously impressed him because he remembered the details sixty years later. Fraternities at that time were certainly taken seriously.

The summer following graduation from the University, DuBose prepared to enter the seminary. In October 1859 he began study at the new diocesan seminary in Camden, South Carolina, as a member of the second class to be admitted at that school. He continued to study there until the outbreak of the war.

### Seminary in Columbia, South Carolina

The first attempt to create a diocesan seminary in South Carolina was in 1857, but not until 1859 was the seminary in Camden opened by Bishop Davis, who would play an important part in DuBose's life during the next decade. The seminary was opened because of a distrust of teaching methods used elsewhere and a desire to train clergy among the people to whom they would be ministering. Most Episcopal seminaries were located in the northeastern United States, and Yankees, even fellow Episcopalians, were not to be trusted. This particular seminary had an extremely short life, principally because the emphasis of the Southern bishops was placed on The University of the South, at Sewanee, Tennessee. Following the end of the war in May, 1865, Bishop Davis spoke these words to the first Convention: "Soon after the passage of Sherman's Army through the country, our Seminary buildings in this place were entirely destroyed by the act of an incendiary. At least two-thirds of the books it contained in it were burnt up. This is to be greatly lamented. To it must be added, I fear, the funds of the Seminary."

The seminary was reopened briefly in October 1866 and then closed permanently in May 1868. The buildings were used to house a girl's school for three years and then sold to Converse College.

DuBose entered the school as one of seven students. Early in his brief tenure at the seminary he visited the home of General Joseph Kershaw, whom DuBose discovered was a distant relative of his as "representatives of the Camden branch of our family, the Isaac DuBoses."[7] This fortuitous relationship was to be important to DuBose during the coming war, as well in later life.

Unfortunately, once again, DuBose's health began to trouble him. He developed an "obstinate cough, which I could not get rid of and which held on for a long time after." To shake the cough, DuBose left for an extended camping trip through the mountains of North Carolina. During this series of trips, he became acquainted with the lady who was to become his wife, Miss Anne Barnwell (Nannie) Peronneau. Miss Peronneau was apparently camping with her family in the same area as were DuBose and his friends. DuBose does not mention who his companions were, but I would speculate that he was with some of his "extended family," and these folks knew no strangers. DuBose must have fallen hard, because for the next couple of years he managed to plan many vacations, trips and furloughs near the location where Miss Nannie happened to be at the time. DuBose returned to the Seminary in Camden in the fall of 1860.

# Chapter III

"Secession – Treason or States Rights?"

# CIVIL WAR: BACKGROUND AND THE BEGINNING
## (1861)

The Citadel, circa 1855
Courtesy, The Citadel Archives

# CHAPTER III

## CIVIL WAR: The Background and the Beginning

### Synopsis

DuBose entered the Civil War period representing the "upper-crust" of the plantation owners in the Low Country of South Carolina. His family owned several plantations and the slaves needed for the cotton-based agricultural business. When DuBose left the academic atmosphere in which he had lived a protected life, he was prepared for the part of an officer of the Confederacy, complete with personal body servant. He was well educated with a bachelor's degree from the premier military college of South Carolina, The Citadel, along with several post-graduate "certificates" from the University of Virginia. He had spent one and one-half years in the seminary preparing for the Episcopal priesthood. But he was yanked back into the secular world to defend his state and his country. He held the popular views of the day for a person of his class in life: sexist, racist, and elitist. His views were the same as those that led up to the war and influenced the conduct and ultimate conclusion of it.

## The Background

The South in which DuBose lived in the years leading up to the Civil War was rural, as described by a British visitor in 1856: "Every step one takes in the South, one is struck with the rough look of the whole civilization. Towns and villages are few and far between." Large cities were rare; in the South only New Orleans with a population of 150,000 was near to comparable in size and diversity to the larger cities in the North. This rural landscape, together with the slow agricultural life and the lack of progressive industry, were exactly what Southerners, at least the well-to-do, wanted in this time before the War.

### *Industrialization and Railroads Vs Agriculture,*

During the time before the Civil War, industrialization of the northeastern United States roared ahead, complete with all the commotion and noise and energy and change in lifestyle caused by such progress. A key factor was the introduction of new machines, many invented by people of the northeastern United States. For example, of 143 important inventions patented in the United States from 1790 to 1860, 93 percent came out of the northern states, mostly from New England. Clearly, the North and the South differed in far more complex than simple compass direction. Because of geography and climate, the northeastern United States was not able to sustain agriculture as a primary way of life and large centers of population became common in that part of the country. New York, Pennsylvania, and Massachusetts were leading manufacturing states, and New York City, Boston, and Philadelphia were the largest industrialized Northern cities.

As the nineteenth century began, cotton was a minor crop. The invention of the cotton gin in the 1790s; the opening up of river bottom lands in Alabama, Mississippi, and Louisiana; and the demand for cotton from overseas combined to make slavery a critical factor in the growing of more cotton. The South was tied to slavery at that point, like it or not. Vested interests developed in slavery, and the agricultural economy, the social system, and slavery were bound together like a Gordian knot. The great majority of Southerners were not slave-holders, and many were nearly as poor as slaves. But slaveholders did not consider themselves sinners, and they convinced the nonslaveholders in the South that emancipation would produce economic ruin.

The South remained dependent on a plantation system that relied on very large scale farming: the 19th century version of large-scale agribusiness. As they were forced to purchase more property when one-crop non-rotation wore out their land, big land owners became bigger. Slave-grown crops such as cotton sustained much of the pre-war growth and territorial expansion for the South. Because of the "twin pillars" of slavery and cotton, that South became more and more distinctly "southern."[10]

The railroads across the United States in the decade before the war grew from 9,000 to 30,000 miles, so that the United States boasted more railways than the rest of the world combined.[10] This expansion in construction of railroads in the United States points out the differing rates in industrialization between the North and the South, a difference that eventually played an important part in the war. Many battles centered around the effort to either keep a railroad operating or to destroy the other side's railroad lines. In 1860 the North had 19,700 completed miles of railroad, and the South (including the border states, most of which remained loyal to the Union and ultimately provided rail transportation to Union armies) had 10,800 miles.[11] This border state factor made the true ratio 23,000 miles in the North to 8,000 in the South. Populations in the two regions were equally disproportionate: the Northern population numbered about 22,336,000 compared with the South's 9,100,000, of which 3,500,000 were black slaves.[12] This disparity prevailed in spite of the fact that the two areas were about equal in size. Twenty-two states were in the North and eleven in the South.

Pre-war Southerners stood for state's rights and a weak national government. They were incensed at the passage of the Fugitive Slave Act of 1850, which gave the federal government substantial additional power in the area of slavery, in which the South felt the federal government should not dabble. Passage of this act led to numerous court tests and trials in the years before the war.

## Secession

The Civil War began politically in December 1860, when DuBose's home state, South Carolina, became the first to react to the election of Abraham Lincoln by seceding from the United States. Living in Camden, only about one hundred miles away from Charleston, DuBose was an eyewitness to all of the exciting events leading up to the war. The citizens of South Carolina, like those of the deep South states and most of the border states, were fearful of the intentions of the first Republican administration toward slavery and the resulting blow that would fall on their slave-based agribusiness-oriented economies. The South Carolinians moved to action, rather than merely talking about it. They moved toward secession from the Union.

### The Act of Secession

On December 19, 1860, 164 men, serving as delegates, traveled from all parts of South Carolina to Charleston to discuss and settle many of the issues regarding the likely secession of the state from the Union. The first choice of a site for the convention of these secessionists was obviously Columbia, the state Capitol. But Columbia was in the throes of a smallpox epidemic and the delegates settled for meeting in the Circular Church in Charleston. A local prominent Union Loyalist, when asked by a visitor for directions to the local insane asylum, pointed to the Baptist Church and said, "that is it–right now, there are 164 insane inmates." In addition to secession, the convention had to consider the laws, customs, and procedures that might be needed to transfer property from the United States to the newly named Commonwealth of South Carolina.

William DuBose, out of the seminary on Christmas vacation, traveled to Charleston. He didn't say why he journeyed there, but it was likely that he wanted to observe the action for himself. He arrived on December 20, 1860, the day on which the order of secession was to be ratified. The ceremony took place that night and the entire city turned out. After spending several days in Charleston, DuBose continued on to visit his grandmother for Christmas. He returned to Camden and stayed until early January, where he heard of the firing of the first shot of the war upon the Northern ship, Star of the West, by cadets of The Citadel.[7]

### Secession–Treason, or States' Rights?

Some Northerners saw secession as no threat, some saw it as a legal impossibility for any state in the Union to secede from a sovereign nation, others saw the need to go to the force of arms to stop this "crime." Whatever the different ways in which people may have seen South Carolina's secession, the act was to lead after only a few months of the two sides "feeling their way" into the deadliest of all American wars. The struggle went on for four long years and eventually killed more than 620,000 young American males (a ratio of roughly one citizen out of every 50). It ultimately proved more lethal than all our other wars combined.

President James Buchanan denounced the illegality of secession, but because the United States had an army of barely 16,000 men at the time, the North could do nothing immediately to prevent the acts of secession by the Southern states. Even worse, in early 1861, most of the 16,000 men in the Union army were scattered in western posts handling the "Indian problem." About one-third of these officers resigned to join the Confederacy. Most of the remaining administrators had been in the army since the War of 1812 and were worn-out bureaucrats.[10]

Most Southerners believed that secession was the ultimate weapon of a state in a federal system. They did not feel that secession was revolutionary but rather that it was the constitutional right of individual states to withdraw from the union which they had helped create. The emerging Confederate nation was in no better shape to wage war than the North. Supplies to build, repair, and run railroads mostly came from Northern factories. The Confederate Quartermaster's Department could never get enough food, tents, clothing, or horses.

The one bright spot was to be the Ordnance Bureau, run by Josiah Gorgas, a person important in William DuBose's later life at The University of the South at Sewanee. At the outset of the war the South had no ordnance plants (with the exception of Tredegar Iron Works in Richmond), no rifle or gunpowder plants. But Gorgas proved to be a wizard at "turning plowshares into swords." During the war, the South suffered from lack of all other types of needed supplies, but it did not suffer for lack of ordnance.[10]

## The Beginning

At six o'clock in the morning of January 9, 1861, The Star of the West approached Fort Sumter in South Carolina with replacement troops and supplies for the Northern troops stationed there. According to the Assistant Adjutant-General of the Union in an order to Major Robert Anderson on January 5, 1861, the Star of the West was amply supplied:

> Two-hundred well-instructed recruits from Fort Columbus. . . , arms for the men, one hundred spare arms and all the cartridges in the arsenal on Governor's Island will be sent; likewise, three month's subsistence for the detachment and six months' desiccated and fresh vegetables, with three or four days' fresh beef for your entire force. Further reinforcements will be sent if necessary.[13]

A South Carolina battery on nearby Morris Island fired two rounds of warning at the Star of the West and was joined by batteries at Fort Moultrie. William DuBose, along with most Charleston residents, saw cadets from The Citadel fire shots at the Union Ship. The battery that fired these shots was commanded by Major P.F. Stevens, at that time superintendent of The Citadel, and eventually to become William DuBose's commanding officer.[6]

### The Beginnings of War–The First Shot

Dickert described the first shot: "The Star of the West. . . laden with supplies for Sumter, had entered the channel with the evident intention of reinforcing Anderson, when The Citadel guards, under Captain Stevens, fired several shots across her bow, then she turned about and sped away to the sea. In the meantime the old battalions of militia had been called out at their respective muster grounds, patriotic speeches made, and a call for volunteers made."[14]

The ship quickly departed, and angry notes were exchanged between South Carolina Governor Francis Pickens and Fort Commander

Major Robert Anderson, a Kentuckian and apparently even a Southern sympathizer. According to the *Confederate Military History*, edited by General Clement A. Evans, at one of the earliest meetings between Anderson and state officials on December 27th, 1860, nine days prior to the shelling, Anderson said, "In this controversy between the North and the South, my sympathies are entirely with the South. These gentlemen (turning to the officers of the post who stood around him) know it perfectly well."[4]

An uneasy truce resulted, but passions and Southern national and state pride spread, and the litany of secession was quickly repeated throughout the South. Mississippi voted to secede the next day (January 9), followed by Florida (January 10), Alabama (January 11), Georgia (January 19), Louisiana (January 26), and Texas (February 1). On February 4, delegates from all these states, except Texas, met at Montgomery, Alabama, to form a provisional government for the Confederate States of America. Five days later Jefferson Davis was named the first (and only) president of the Confederacy.

While waiting for something to happen, volunteers were recruited and companies and regiments organized. Dickert describes the drill training in Charleston that was mandatory for soldiers of that time: "Cadets were sent down from The Citadel as drill masters to all the regiments, and for six hours daily the ears were greeted with 'Hep-hep' to designate the left foot down while on the drill. It took great patience, determination and toil to bring the men under military discipline. Fresh from the fields, shops, and schools, they had been accustomed to the freedom of home life, and with all their patriotism, it took time to break into the harness of military restraint and discipline these lovers of personal freedom."[14]

As early as March 8, 1861, Confederate Brigadier-General G.T. Beauregard stated that although the brigade of state regulars from South Carolina should remain under the pay of South Carolina, they were now under his order and that, "I can perceive among them no spirit of opposition or dissatisfaction. On the contrary, they appear to be animated with the most kindly feelings towards me, and seem highly pleased at the order assigning me to their command."[13] On April 8, 1861, the South Carolina Convention passed an ordinance that transferred to the Confederate Government the use and occupancy of the forts, arsenals, navy yards, custom houses and other public sites within the state.

Three months after the firing on The Star of the West, the shooting began in earnest as Fort Sumter underwent a bombardment by the Confederate Army and Navy that lasted thirty-four hours. A portion of the South Carolina forces firing from Cummings Point was once again commanded by Major P.F. Stevens and included cadets from The Citadel.4 Major Stevens gave details about the activities in his official report, published in *War of the Rebellion*. Stevens discusses the firing of the first shot at 4:00 o'clock on the morning of April 12th and states that his battery immediately joined in and fired on Fort Sumter continuously day and night until the order was given to cease fire on the 13th. Stevens said that is was impossible for him to name all of the officers and men who performed well during the activity, but he gave "great credit . . . to the effective fire of guns directed by officers and men who, with the exception of the officers of the Military Academy, had never until two or three weeks hence undertaken to manage artillery." Stevens' commanding officer, Lieutenant-Colonel Wilmot G. DeSaussure, said in this official report that, "To Maj. P.F. Stevens of The Citadel Academy, I but do justice in saying that by example, by forethought, by energy, by his skill much of the success from this post was achieved. He is entitled to most honorable mention and to the highest praise."[13]      As this first skirmish drew to a close, Union Major Robert Anderson lowered the United States flag and turned the fort over to Confederate officials. The American Civil War had officially begun.

DuBose had again returned from Camden to Charleston to witness the firing upon Fort Sumter. Together with a considerable percentage of the residents of Charleston:

> I paraded the long walk of the Battery until a very late hour awaiting the shot that should open the direct attack upon Fort Sumter by the South Carolina forces. The shot did not come until three or four o'clock the next morning, and the city were all asleep in their beds.[7]

The Northern press was unanimous as to the brevity of the "supposed war." In general, it wrote that a few months was the maximum time anyone could possibly expect before the "rebellion" would be ended, the traitors hanged, the ragamuffins scattered, and the rebellious states returned to the Union from which they had absolutely no business leaving in the first place. In retrospect, of course, the Northern crystal ball was unfortunately clouded.

The Southern personal and editorial approach to forecasting the length of the war was equally incorrect. Only the veterans, the men who had seen war before, could have speculated that the war might possibly last more than a few months, much less the four bloody years that ensued.

### Northern Journalistic Views of the War

Following are selected examples of the editorials common in Northern newspapers during the time period between the firing on Fort Sumter and the commencing of full-scale war.

#### The New York Tribune, 1861

"The Rebellion is nothing more or less than the natural recourse of all mean-spirited and defeated tyrannies to rule or ruin, making, of course, a wide distinction between the will and power, for the hanging of traitors is sure to begin before one month is over. The Nations of Europe may rest assured that Jeff. Davis & Co. will be swinging from the battlements at Washington, at least, by the 4th of July. We spit upon a later and longer deferred justice."

### The New York Times, 1861

"Let us make quick work. The 'rebellion' as some people designate it, is an unborn tadpole. Let us not fall into the delusion . . . of mistaking a 'local commotion' for a revolution. A strong active 'pull together' will do our work effectually in thirty days. We have only to send a column of 25,000 men across the Potomac to Richmond, and burn out the rats there; another column of 25,000 to Cairo, seizing the cotton ports of the Mississippi; and retaining the remaining 25,000, included in Mr. Lincoln's call for 75,000 men, at Washington, not because there is need for them there, but because we do not require their services elsewhere."

### The Philadelphia Press, 1861

"No man of sense could, for a moment, doubt that this much-ado-about-nothing would end in a month. The Northern people are 'simply invincible.' The rebels, a mere band of ragamuffins, will fly, like chaff before the wind, on our approach."

### The Chicago Tribune, 1861

"Let the East get out of the way; this is a war of the West. We can fight the battle, and successfully, within two or three months at the furthest. Illinois can whip the South by herself. We insist on the matter being turned over to us."

### Southern Opinions about the War

The following is from Stern: "The young volunteers thought one good battle would settle the whole matter; and, indeed, after First Manassas many thought they might as well go home! The whole North was frightened, and no more armies would dare assail the soil of Old Virginia . . . The newspaper men delighted in telling the soldiers that the Yankees were a diminutive race, of feeble constitution, timid as hares, with no enthusiasm, and that they would perish in short order under the glow of our Southern sun . . . Many feared the war would end before they would have a fair chance to make a record, and that when the war was over they would have to sit by, dumb, and hear the fortunate ones, who had smelt the battle, tell to admiring home circles the story of the bloody field. Most of these got in in time to satisfy their longings . . ."[15]

Confederate Sam Watkins in his ground-level view of the war, *Co. Aytch*, discusses his service with the Maury County, Tennessee "Grays." The book, prepared from his wartime diary, discusses the fiery Southern secession speeches he heard before the war: "Flags made by the ladies were presented to companies, and to hear the young orators tell of how they would protect that flag or come not at all, and if they fell they would fall with their backs to the field and their feet to the foe, would fairly make our hair stand on end with intense patriotism, and we wanted to march right off and whip twenty Yankees. But we soon found out that the glory of war was at home among the ladies and not upon the field of blood and carnage and death, where our comrades were mutilated and torn by shot and shell."[16]

The South entered the war in the spring of 1861 in high spirits. The people were convinced of the rightness of their cause and the necessity for defense of their homeland; they were also sure of success. They felt that Southerners were outside people who were accustomed to riding, shooting, and hard work. Yankees, by contrast, were soft, pale, shop-born indoors people who would run at the first shots. Certainty of success in the war effort was shown in southern elementary textbooks for the children. For example, Johnson's *Elementary Arithmetic*, published in North Carolina, posed the following questions for the children: "(1) A Confederate soldier captured 8 Yankees each day for 9 successive days; how many did he capture in all? (2) If one Confederate soldier can kill 90 Yankees how many Yankees can 10 Confederate soldiers kill? (3) If one Confederate soldier can whip 7 Yankees, how many soldiers can whip 49 Yankees?"[17]

The military strategy of the Civil War was drastically different from that used today. Many civilians of that day (and of today) could hardly understand the impossibility of one army completely wiping out the other in a battle during the Civil War. Primacy in this war would result from defense and retreat, not from obliteration of the enemy in a single, decisive battle. The way for the North to win was through the slow process of conquering the territory of the Southern states by using overwhelming numbers of fighting men and seemingly endless quantities of supplies.

The logistical strategy followed by the North was aimed at weakening and depleting the Southern army by depriving them of transportation, weapons, horses, recruits, food, and fodder. In the long run it was a successful strategy that eventually ended the brutal war. Although leaders of the North thought in terms of a limited war of attrition, with goals to surpress the insurrection and win back loyalty of the South, the conflict became far more than a limited war. It was a total war that required mobilization of vast resources, including men, as well as the destruction of vast resources, including men. Eventually 620,000 men would lose their lives (360,000 Union men and 260,000 Confederates).

### More About Railroads

Railroads during the Civil War were both critical and vulnerable. Loosening a rail would cause a train to leave the tracks, and the burning of a bridge or trestle would stop service until repairs were made. The 30-plus miles per hour speed of the railroads meant quicker delivery than by wagons even over the best roads. High water and mud were also not the problem for rail traffic that they were for wagons and teams of horses or mules. Because of both of the existing and hurriedly constructed railroads, armies could operate from bases of supply well away from the action.

The importance of the railroad to both Northern and Southern armies cannot be overemphasized. General Order Number 7, July 20, 1862, by Colonel George D. Ruggles, Chief of Staff for Major-General Pope of the Northern Army, gives a feel for the criticality of the railroads by describing the Union approach to solving the problem of sabotage, which required punishment not only of the saboteurs but also of the people who lived in the area where the deed was done: "The people of the valley of the Shenandoah, and throughout the region of operations of this army, living along the lines of railroad and telegraph, and along the routes of travel in rear of the United States forces, are notified that they will be held responsible for any injury done to the track, line, or road, or for any attacks upon trains or straggling soldiers by bands of guerrillas in their neighborhood... It is, therefore, ordered that whenever a railroad, wagon-road, or telegraph is injured by parties of guerrillas, the citizens living within five miles of the spot shall be turned out in mass to repair the damage, and shall, besides, pay the United States, in money or in property, to be levied by military force, the full amount of the pay and subsistence of the whole force necessary to coerce the performance of the work during the time occupied in completing it . . ."[13]

### Military Tactics and Marching

The identical military tactics used by both the Union and Confederate armies in 1861 were from French Army manuals. Both armies were organized with the company of 50 men as the basic infantry unit. The armies then formed a regiment of ten companies, a brigade of two to five regiments, a division of two to five brigades, and a corps of two or more divisions. For ease in following use of the names of these differing groups of soldiers, Figure 1 provides an approximation of the organization of the two major armies of the Civil War, the Army of Virginia and the Army of the Potomac. Information for this figure comes from Jones.[18]

Regiments marched on roads in columns and, when headed for battle, often marched across the countryside in compact formations from which they could quickly deploy into one or more lines of soldiers of two rows each. These lines were the fighting formation, because in this layout the largest number of soldiers could fire rifles or muskets. Very few soldiers engaged in long-range fire, because of the difficult terrain on which most Civil War battles were fought and also because of inaccurate firing by many of the weapons of the day. This was particularly true in the first few years of the war. The defender in a battle enjoyed an advantage over the attacker, because the defender could kneel behind rock walls or earthen breastworks and deliver more accurate fire. After the war began to drag on and patriotic fervor cooled as survival desire increased, most soldiers gladly would have given up the patriotic thrill of charging the enemy with flags flying and rebel yell (or equivalent) ringing for the security of lying behind a rock wall and carefully aiming their weapons at a charging enemy.

During the fighting in Civil War battles, rarely were all of the troops on either side engaged in actual fighting on a battlefield or in a skirmish. Some were held back as reserves and not brought into action unless needed. Some were detached from the action and used to guard important trains, wagons, roads, or bridges. Some were posted for a possible attack that may or may not have ever come. Other troops may have been in the area of the battlefield, but by circumstances of the flow of battle or of topography, they remained untouched while units all around suffered large numbers of casualties. These troops were used as a reforming line for fighting troops that were in the thick of battle and had lost men.

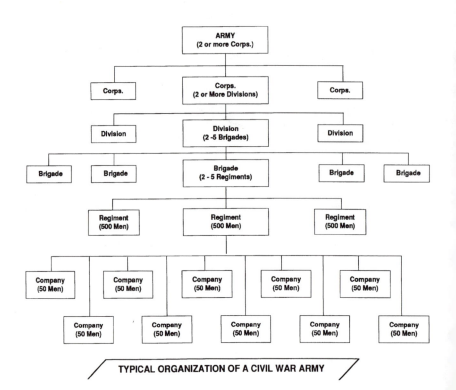

**TYPICAL ORGANIZATION OF A CIVIL WAR ARMY**

The general officers in both armies during the Civil War led their troops by example. In combat, for the most part, they led from the front, not the rear. They were more successful leaders when they promoted "do as I do, not as I say do," rather than the reverse. In the armies of both South and North, the proportion of officers killed in action was about fifteen percent higher than the proportion of enlisted men killed. Generals suffered the highest combat casualties; their chances of death in battle were fifty percent greater than those of a private.10 Officers on both sides began to stay off horses, and many began to wear nondescript uniforms with only the barest proof of rank. Sharpshooters particularly liked to shoot officers, which explains why officers had such a substantially higher death rate than the other men. There are those with differing opinions; for example, Sam Watkins writes "he would shoot the ones that were shooting at him."[16]

Marching was required for the movement of troops in preparation for the next battle. What was it like for the average footsoldier? One of the best descriptions of the visual impact of marching armies is by David L. Thompson, Company G, 9th New York Volunteers: "By daylight next morning we were in motion again–the whole army. The gathering of such a multitude is a swarm, its march a vast migration. It fills up every road leading in the same direction over a breadth of many miles, with long ammunition and supply trains . . . infantry and artillery next in order outwardly, feelers of cavalry all along its front and far out on its flanks; while behind, trailing along every road for miles . . . are the rabble of stragglers-laggards through sickness or exhaustion, squads of recruits, convalescents from the hospital . . . Stand, now, by the roadside while a corps is filing past. They march 'route step', as it is called–that is, not keeping time–and four abreast . . . If the march has just begun, you hear the sound of voices everywhere, with roars of laughter in spots, marking the company wag . . . Later on, when the weight of knapsack and musket begins to tell, those sounds die out; a sense of weariness and labor rises from the toiling masses streaming by . . . So uniformly does the mass move on that it suggests a great machine, requiring only its directing mind. Yet such a mass, without experience in battle, would go to pieces before a moderately effective fire . . . Here is the secret of organization–the aim and crown of drill, to make the units one, that when the crisis comes, the missile may be thoroughly compacted. Too much, however, has been claimed for theoretic discipline–not enough for intelligent individual action. No remark was oftener on the lips of officers during the war than this; 'Obey orders! I do your thinking for you.' But that soldier is the best whose good sense tells him when to be merely a part of a machine and when not."[19]

Sam Watkins in *Co. Aytch* felt differently about his unimportance as a cog in the machine. Some of his bitterness regarding the role of the foot-soldier came from the fact that late in the war, he participated in the Battle of Franklin, Tennessee. That battle is regarded as a glaring example of a situation where a commander's ego and ill-preparedness forced his foot-soldiers into the role of providing target practice for the opposing troops located behind unassailable breastworks. The soldier was truly a cog in the machine at that battle. Watkins stated his understanding of the task and the role of the ordinary footsoldier as follows: "A private soldier is but an automaton, a machine that works by the command of a good, bad, or indifferent engineer, and is presumed to know nothing of all these great events. His business is to load and shoot, stand picket, videt, etc., while the officers sleep, or perhaps die on the field of battle and glory, and his obituary and epitaph but 'one' remembered among the slain, but to what company, regiment or corps he belongs, there is no account- he is soon forgotten."[16]

Watkins' and Thompson's views of the role of the common foot-soldier are truly opposed. In his fighting days DuBose, an officer from the old-school tradition, would have believed that the soldier was to do exactly as told. Did this view change during his chaplaincy? I suspect his concern for his fellow man grew and expanded immensely during this period of his life. His story about some foreign-born soldiers whom he was ordered to prepare for execution very late in the war clearly illustrates his compassion. I believe that his response to "do precisely as you are told" probably began to temper during this time as his concern for the soldiers to whom he was ministering grew.

# Chapter IV

"...a time to try the soul, the balls whizzing past
and men falling around."
– South Carolina soldier
after the Battle of Kingston

## WILLIAM PORCHER DUBOSE AS A SOLDIER
### (1861-1863)

W.P. DuBose in his Confederate Uniform–Likely a
modified Citadel cadet jacket
Courtesy The University of the South Archives

# CHAPTER IV

# WILLIAM P. DUBOSE AS A SOLDIER

## Synopsis

William Porcher DuBose spent the next year in the thick of front line war action in the eastern theater (the extent of his travels from the beginning of the war November 21, 1861, to Second Manassas, August 30, 1862, is shown in Figure 2). His unit was in the midst of the Second Battle of Manassas. Between one-half and two-thirds of the Holcombe Legion, men DuBose had gone to school with, drilled with, and fought alongside of since the inception of the war, were dead or wounded or missing in action. DuBose himself was wounded twice in this battle. He was placed in charge of the Legion following the battle–a tough assignment because less than one hundred men and few officers were left to be organized. A lieutenant was not often placed in command of an entire regiment. However, under his leadership the Legion sucessfully made a brutal march from Manassas to one of the gaps through South Mountain in Maryland. The march was accomplished in spite of little food, medicine, or doctors. The men's clothing and shoes were in abominable shape.

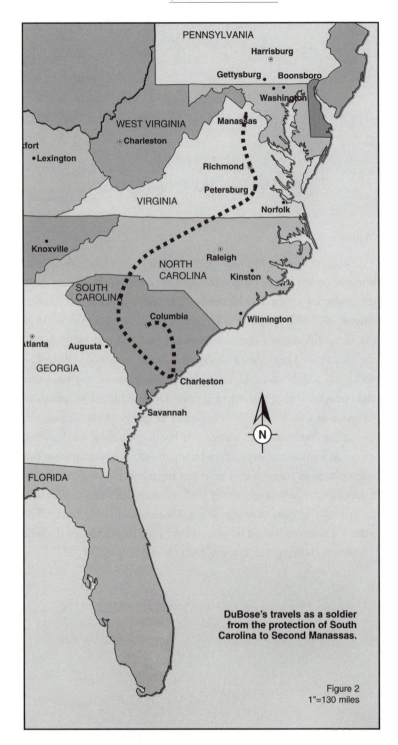

DuBose's travels as a soldier
from the protection of South
Carolina to Second Manassas.

Figure 2
1"=130 miles

While conducting a reconnaissance at General Lee's request after the Battle of South Mountain, DuBose was captured. He was incarcerated at Union prison camp Fort Delaware and later paroled and released under the "one for one" prisoner exchange rule early in the war. After recuperating at Winnsboro he returned to his unit in time to fight at the Battle for the Bridges at Kinston, North Carolina, where he received his most serious wound. The Legion then went to the Jackson-Vicksburg, Mississippi, area to face Grant and his army. While DuBose was at this post he received notification of his appointment as Chaplain.

## Protection of South Carolina

Soon after William DuBose's return to the seminary in Camden, the war began in earnest. The coast of South Carolina was thought to be open to invasion by the Federal Navy or Army. According to DuBose, "Gunboats infested it (the coast), and threatened the important railway connection between Charleston and Savannah, which ran along the coast. Governor Pickens determined to organize a command of State troops for State defense."[7]

In 1861 the Holcombe Legion was formed by Governor Francis W. Pickens to protect South Carolina's coastline and railroads. This regiment was named Holcombe after the maiden name of Pickens' wife. The Legion consisted of a regiment of infantry and a battalion each of cavalry and artillery.[6] The Citadel organized the Legion. Colonel Peter Fayssoux Stevens, former Commandant of The Citadel was in command and F. Gendron Palmer was named major. William Porcher DuBose was appointed lieutenant and adjutant of the Legion by Governor Pickens on November 21, 1861.

DuBose was part of the Infantry Regiment of the Holcombe Legion, South Carolina Volunteers, Elliott's Brigade, Johnson's Division, Anderson's Corps, in the Army of Northern Virginia. The Holcombe Legion had a cavalry battalion attached to them until March 18, 1864, when it was separated from the Legion and increased to a regiment, later to be designated the 7th Regiment South Carolina Cavalry. The entire Legion was also known at times as the South Carolina Volunteers.[20]

In 1861 the Legion was mustered out of the State of South Carolina service into the service of the Confederate States of America. This process began on November 8, 1861, the day after Port Royal was taken and General Robert E. Lee took command of the military departments of Georgia and South Carolina by order of Jefferson

Davis, President of the Confederate States of America. For DuBose, 1861 was also an important year for personal reasons: in April of that year, he was engaged to Anne Barnwell (Nannie) Peronneau of Charleston.

### The Citadel–A Key to the Confederacy

The new commandant of the Holcombe Legion, Major P.F. Stevens, had been Commander of The Citadel until August 6, 1861, when he resigned to follow a call to the ministry. Stevens graduated from The Citadel in 1849 and worked his way up the ranks after graduation, eventually serving as Professor of Mathematics. He was promoted to Captain in 1856 and taught ethics, French, and belles-lettres. In 1858 he added Astronomy to his courses. In 1859 Stevens attempted to resign, but the board refused to accept his resignation and instead made him Commander of The Citadel as a major, teaching civil and military engineering. When the coast of South Carolina was threatened by Federal gunboats in 1861, Stevens offered his services to Governor Pickens. He commanded the Legion until the Battle of Sharpsburg, where he received an arm wound. Then he again resigned to return to the ministry.[21]

The Citadel was an important resource to the Confederacy. Out of the 224 eligible, active and present students, 209 entered Confederate service. Forty-nine of these died in the service of their country, joining the total list of 200 former cadets who died in the war. The students and graduates of The Citadel were recognized as good military leaders, and many became officers up to the rank of Brigadier General.[21]

The Citadel was intimately involved in the war from the beginning; her laboratory became the first Confederate test grounds for ordnance. It was put into full operation and supplied military necessities to the South. Following the end of the war, the buildings of The Citadel were occupied and used by the victorious Northern authorities while enforcing Reconstruction. In 1882 The Citadel reopened its doors as an institution of higher education and has remained open since.

The forming of the Holcombe Legion and the call to DuBose to serve as lieutenant and adjutant forced him to make the decision to leave the seminary at once to take part in organizing and disciplining the Legion. Because DuBose was in preparation for the ministry, he was required to wait for permission from the Bishop of the diocese. This wait apparently caused DuBose's father (Theodore Samuel DuBose) anxiety. He wanted his sons to participate in the war as soon as possible. Even though he felt that education should be a primary goal for the Southern gentleman, defense of one's home and ideals was even more important. William's father wanted to be personally involved in the war, like most of the adult male South Carolinians, but because of his age and his responsibilities at the plantations, he was unable to do so. I suggest that the philosophy of the time was that the next best thing to defending the Southern way of life is to have your son or sons participate for you.

Theodore Samuel DuBose, however, set himself to the task of equipping his son for the service. The plantation had been its own supplier in peacetime and was definitely up to the task in wartime. The selection of a horse was foremost and Samuel turned to the family to provide the best available–an offspring of a line of horses from Red Doe, a horse that became famous during the Revolutionary War. William DuBose described his pride in the personal equipment with which he went off to war as follows (probably fairly typical for the sons of South Carolina plantation owners):

> He (DuBose's Father) sent me down a set of military trappings for my horse, which was rather exceptional in its quality and style . . . Archie (DuBose's uncle's horse) was over twenty years of age, but as young as ever in temper and spirit and appearance. The other Red Doe horse was a magnificent animal, quite young and representing the very best of the stock in appearance. My Uncle offered me my choice of either of these two horses. I took Archie. The

trappings my father had sent fitted very beautifully and were a matter of great pride and joy to me . . . When my father equipped me for the service the most touching item of the outfit was a bodyservant in the person of Stephen. Stephen had always been in the house. We children had been accustomed to him all our lives and were scarcely aware of the treasure we had in him. *But* my father and mother *knew* and valued him very deeply and so in fact we all did . . . Stephen was the least pretentious of servants, silent and undemonstrative; but in him was the most devoted and loyal spirit and heart.[7]

So DuBose was prepared to go to war with a horse that was over twenty years old, and a body servant, Stephen, who was relatively aged. DuBose said that his father told him that " . . . Stephen's health had not been very good and he thought camp life might be of service to him."[7] DuBose read between the lines that his father meant for William to be in "trusty hands." DuBose's horse and body servant were both of an age where retirement might have been appropriate, but here they were going off to war. This is a good example of the opinions of most Southerners, both at home and off to war, who did not expect the conflict to last long. William's father probably felt that a short change of pace might be good for both the horse and the servant.[7]

Cheshire, in *The Church in the Confederate States,* briefly discussed the role of the slave/servant who faithfully served his officer/master during the war. The tone of the comment has to be considered in light of the general attitudes in the South at the time of the Civil War.

"A word should be said of a very faithful class of Negroes, those who accompanied their masters to the War. The personal bond between master and servant in this case was particularly close, and the latter very often showed an almost maternal care and solicitude in providing for the

comfort and welfare of his master. With every opportunity of escaping to the enemy, where freedom was assured,
there were very few instances of it."[22]

Cheshire's comments held true for DuBose. DuBose told several stories about the close relationship he had with Stephen in the early
parts of the war. He also said that the men who served in the mess
quickly learned of Stephen's qualities. A fighting man always appreci-
ates help with the more mundane parts of warlife–cooking, washing,
tent-setting and striking, etc. Later in the war, when DuBose became
engaged to be married, he neglected to tell Stephen directly, and
Stephen's feelings were hurt. This was a mistake that DuBose hurried
to correct.

The Holcombe Legion was stationed on the west side of the
Ashley River in Charleston to protect the city and the coastal railroad
line. DuBose said that he and the Legion spent the fall and winter of
1861/1862 in hard drill and discipline, in skirmishing with gunboats,
and " . . . in the occasional more romantic experiences of camp life."[6]

I'm not exactly sure what DuBose meant by that statement. As a
student at The Citadel in Charleston, he undoubtedly became
immersed in the flow of social life in that city. He, as the other soldiers in Charleston for the defense of South Carolina, had substantial
free time in the early days of the war and probably spent some of it
visiting friends and relatives who lived in the area. In addition, soldier
life in long-term camp before shots are fired, is much like scout camp;
campfires with singing, drill and manuvers, and meeting other men
from all walks of life.

### First Expedition of the Holcombe Legion

On January 25, 1862, the Holcombe Legion was involved in a foray in the area of Adams Run. In a report from Brigadier General N.G. Evans to the Assistant Adjutant-General in Charleston, Evans, in the racist attitude of the South at that time, gave the following report, "I have the honor to report that the expedition under Col. P.F. Stevens, Holcombe Legion, has succeeded in capturing about 50 Negroes on Edisto Island, several of whom are the Negroes who attacked my pickets at Watt's Cut. I think after a due investigation, should any of the Negroes be convicted, they should be hanged as soon as possible at some public place as an example. The Negroes had evidently been incited to insurrection by the enemy. I have now as prisoners several Negroes, who say they can identify the men who attacked the pickets. I will keep all the Negroes until the investigation is through, and would earnestly request instructions from the general commanding. The Negro fellows not implicated directly I propose to iron heavily and work them under guard on the causeway now being made at Church Flats. Colonel Stevens will probably arrive today with the remainder of the Negroes."[13]

On February 15, 1862, the Holcombe Legion was still in the vicinity of Adams Run, as mentioned in a report from General Evans to Assistant Adjutant-General Taylor in Savannah, Georgia. In that report the Legion is described as 492 strong and located between Togodo and Willstown, opposite Jehossee Island.[13]

According to Evans, Colonel P.F. Stevens was in charge of an attempt to capture the Federal guard on Little Edisto Island and to make a reconnaissance on the main island on March 29, 1862. On the 28th of March, the entire Legion, composed at that time of 343 infantry and 75 dismounted cavalry, crossed the Dawho River on a bridge of flats at approximately 3:00 A.M. Near Old Dominion the enemy's pickets first challenged the Legion and shots were exchanged. When a larger force, which included artillery, was discovered, Colonel Stevens decided to retreat across the long causeway. Even after several firefights it still took a struggle to break through to the causeway. The Legion retreated across the bridge and burned it behind them. Stevens and his men, particularly Major Palmer, were commended by their commanding officer for skill and gallantry exhibited during the skirmish.[4]

DuBose mentions in his *Reminiscences* that this first camp was just over the Ashley River in St. Andrews Parish, a short ride from Charleston. The camp was soon moved to the neighborhood of Adams Run, some twenty miles from the city, where the men were in " . . . constant alarm and actual contact with the gunboats penetrating the waters and threatening the railway connections."[7] DuBose tells an amusing story of one of his confrontations with the "Yankees," again from his *Reminiscences*:

> Another time I was sent (one of two) to reconnoiter and see if the enemy were on the island. The island had been very deeply ditched across–a deep ditch and a high bank on one side. The road passed over that ditch and was the only break to it and we couldn't see behind the high bank without taking the road, exposed to the enemies' fire should they be behind the ditch. The road, near the ditch, passed over a little tide-water stream and as we were on the bridge of this stream we suddenly heard the click of a gun. The ditch and the bank were just a few feet in front of us. Of course it halted us with a start. There we stood, expecting every minute the shot to follow the click. While we stood there waiting, another click came and revealed the source and character of it. It was from one of those little fiddlers (crab), a little animal that abounds in the tidewater. The water sometimes gets in them and the bubble bursts with a sound for all the world like the click of a gun. We felt rather let-down from the tragic attitude we had occupied before, expecting every moment to be shot. The Yankees were not there.[7]

The death of his father added a sad note to the spring of 1862. Infected with measles while ministering to sick soldiers, Mr. DuBose could not recover. Because most of the young soldiers were from rural areas and had little contact with "civilized" diseases like measles, tens of thousands died from this seemingly innocuous illness. William DuBose returned home for a brief time at his father's death. The timing of this visit proved fortunate because the visit was the last he had with his mother. She died soon afterward, after long years of poor health. DuBose identified her illness as consumption (author's note: tuberculosis?) and he spoke tenderly of his mother in later years:

> She was always delicate, but it never interfered with her efficiency and above all things with her beautiful control of the house, her children and her servants. I can remember her with her invariable sweetness, also her strength in the discipline of servants and children, and with her little (in the last days) first grandchildren around her. She no more spoiled them than she had spoiled her own children. I declare, I remember that with those little grandchildren, she was just as positive and inflexible in making them obey![7]

During the summer of 1862, DuBose submitted two requisitions that are included in his military records in the State of South Carolina Archives. On May 28th, he requested one wall tent, which he stated was for his orderlies, who to that point in time had not been issued one. On August 11th, DuBose requisitioned still another wall tent with the following explanation: "I certify that the above requisition is correct; and that the articles specified are absolutely requisite for the public service, rendered so by the following circumstances: that the tent which I at present occupy has been condemned as unfit for use by a board of officers (see report of board of survey No. 1, Plate 3)." It is hard to imagine a tent in such awful condition that it had to be condemned! During April, May, and June, 1862, DuBose and the Holcombe Legion were still listed with Confederate troops stationed in South Carolina.[13]

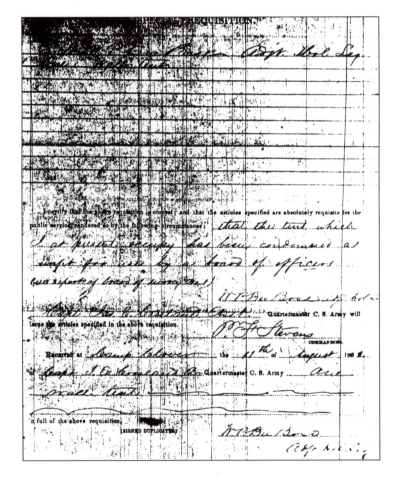

## Northern Virginia

**Holcombe Legion goes to War**

In July of 1862, the Holcombe Legion was fully mustered into Confederate service and ordered north to Virginia to join the forces of Robert E. Lee and Stonewall Jackson in defense of Richmond. The official order came on July 17th to Brigadier-General Evans at Adams Run, South Carolina, from Major-General J.C. Pemberton. The order stated that the Holcombe Legion, along with three other regiments of infantry and one of artillery, was to "proceed at once to Richmond, Virginia." Pemberton contacted Adjutant S. Cooper in Richmond with the expected departure dates of the various regiments being sent to help Richmond. In his July 20th communication he says that the Holcombe Legion would probably leave Charleston on July 21st.[13]

DuBose took advantage of the time provided by the confusion of the date of the departure from Charleston after mustering into the service of the Army of Virginia. He retired his aging faithful horse, Archie, and replaced him with another, because he had

> . . . too much regard for Archie's age to take him with me and sent him carefully home to Ophir where I thought I knew he would receive the most devoted attention for the rest of his life, for few horses have been so beloved, but I am sorry to have to relate, that in the last days of the war, when Charleston had to be abandoned and the country was overcome by the enemy, Archie fell into their hands and we know nothing more of his fate.[7]

The Legion arrived at the close of the Seven Days Campaign (June 25 to July 1, 1862) and fought several small skirmishes with the Federal forces stationed there. They first saw battle during General McClellan's unsuccessful assault on the defenses of Richmond when General Lee first assumed command of the Army of Northern Virginia. After Malvern Hill, the Legion was next sent to Gordonsville under General Lee's command to meet the advance of Union General John Pope, then to the Rappahannock to dispute that crossing by Federal troops, and then on to the Plains of Manassas.

Apparently, the Legion was moving rapidly and their supply wagons could not keep up (author's note: I suspect that DuBose experienced de ja' vu back to the time when The Citadel made their summer march and left all their provisionary wagons behind). DuBose says of the time during the Gordonsville campaign, "I was not under a roof, not even under the cover of a tent until I was safely housed (as a wounded prisoner) in Fort Delaware."[7] It was also at this time that DuBose managed to find himself a replacement for his horse, Archie. DuBose tells of an evening when he and another soldier with the Legion were some distance from the camp. They expected no trouble so neither of them carried any arms. They ran into a heavily armed cavalryman, but it was too dark to see his uniform. When the stranger asked DuBose and his companion where a certain Yankee regiment was, they pointed him in a direction away from themselves. As he turned to look down the road, the two Confederates took him prisoner and the surprised Yankee surrendered his carbine, pistol, sword, and himself to the unarmed Confederates. DuBose dryly states that, "As I had not yet secured a replacement for Archie, his horse also came in very well."[7]

## Second Manassas (Bull Run) August 30, 1862

The first major battle of the Civil War and a second major one were fought at the same location in Northern Virginia, just a few miles from Washington. These two battles have always been known by different names by the Northern and Southern combatants, a situation true of a number of Civil War battles. The South named the battle after the nearest small town (and more importantly to their well-being, the railroad junction), Manassas Junction. The North named the battlefield Bull Run, after the small stream that was crossed and re-crossed many times by the two armies during both battles.

On August 30th of 1862, DuBose was wounded twice during the Confederate victory at the Second Battle of Manassas (Second Bull Run). Here his horse was shot. At the close of the battle he was the only field officer of the Holcombe Legion who was able to fight through the battle. The Holcombe Legion is listed in the Official Records as a part of Evans' Brigade for the battles of August 28-September 1, 1862. In that same reference Surgeon Lafayette Guild of the Confederate Medical Director's staff, reports that in the Holcombe Legion 24 men were killed and 131 were wounded; a total of 155 men were out of action.[13]

### Manassas Vs Bull Run Battles

The prize fought over by the armies at both Manassas battles was the railroad. The railroad depot at Manassas Junction was only a few miles south of Bull Run Creek. All of the rail-carried troops and supplies bound north from Richmond to the Confederate front necessarily passed through this intersection. Manassas Junction was the key to the Manassas Railroad, which led to the Shenandoah Valley. That valley was important for its agricultural production as well as for providing the most logical path for armies heading south or north. The Confederates desperately needed to keep Manassas Junction open and operating. According to Confederate General G.T. Beauregard, ". . . it had a railroad approach

in its rear for the easy accumulation of reinforcements and all the necessary munitions of war from the southward, at the same time another (the
Manassas Gap) railway, diverging laterally to the left from that point, gave
rapid communications with the fertile valley of the Shenandoah, then
teeming with live stock and cereal subsistence, as well as with other
resources essential to the Confederates . . . during the period of accumulation, seasoning, and training, it might be fed from the fat fields, pas-
tures, and garners of Loudoun, Fauquier, and the Lower Shenandoah
Valley counties, which otherwise must have fallen into the hands of the
enemy."[20]

Visualizing the physical setting at Manassas enhances our understanding of the battle. Pollard gives the following description; "Bull Run
constitutes the northern boundary of that county which it divides from
Fairfax; and on its memorable banks, about three miles to the northwest
of the junction of the Manassas Gap with the Orange and Alexandria railroad, was fought the gallant action of the 18th of July (author's note-
1861). It is a small stream, running in this locality, nearly from west to east,
to its confluence with the Occoquan River, about twelve miles from the
Potomac, and draining a considerable scope of country, from its source in
Bull Run Mountain to within a short distance of the Potomac at Occoquan.
Roads traverse and intersect the surrounding country in almost every
direction. The banks of the stream are rocky and steep, but abound in
long-used fords."[23]

The Second Battle of Manassas, like the first, is considered to have
been a Southern victory. The battle, when combined with the rest of the
three-week campaign, cost the Northern army 14,462 men (approximately 24 percent of their force) and the Southern army 9,474 men (approximately 19 percent of their force.)[24] The battle pointed out the superiori-
ty of Southern military leadership in the early part of the war. For example, Union Major General John Pope had several opportunities to crush
Lee's divided army in the days immediately preceding Second Manassas,
but tentative leadership allowed General Lee to bring his troops back
together at Manassas; the result was a reversal and a complete rout.
President Lincoln, highly disillusioned after the battle, merged Pope's
Army of Virginia with the Army of the Potomac and reluctantly restored
McClellan (also an extremely tentative leader) to command.

DuBose, with the Holcombe Legion, reached Richmond early in August, 1862, a short time after the Battle of Richmond.[4] They had several skirmishes with the Federal troops remaining in the Richmond vicinity. From there, on the way to Manassas, they encamped several days near Gordonsville. The Legion left on Saturday and arrived at the Rappahannock River where they again skirmished with the enemy. A shell blast in DuBose's area scattered shrapnel in the midst of the Legion; one piece struck DuBose in the knee, " . . . nearly breaking the bone and laming me for sometime." DuBose recalled that the artillery piece " . . . which we were supporting, had reached the top of the hill, when it was literally blown off by shells from the opposite side of the river."[7]

On October 13, 1862, at General Lee's request, General Nathan Evans wrote a summary of the battles of Rappahannock Station and Second Manassas. In this report he says " . . . the brave and energetic Major F.G. Palmer, of the Holcombe Legion . . . " was among the wounded; and "To Col. P.F. Stevens, of the Holcombe Legion, commanding the brigade, I am much indebted for his untiring zeal and dauntless courage, cheering his men under heavy fire during the entire engagement."[13] Also on October 13, Colonel Stevens described the Battle of Rappahannock Station (the battle in which DuBose was slightly wounded) as follows:

> On August 23, last, at an early hour of the morning, my regiment was put into position near where the Orange and Alexandria Railroad crosses the Rappahannock . . . I moved forward, crossed the stream under a fire of grape and canister, and advanced to the top of the hill. The works were found deserted, but bearing fresh evident signs of recent occupation, such as tools in the trenches, fresh meat, etc. Scarcely had we gained the hill when a heavy fire was opened upon it from several batteries . . . Later in the afternoon our batteries opened fire on the right, and the enemy not replying, I sent forward a detachment of skirmishers . . . who found the enemy gone . . . After burying my dead, I returned to camp.[13]

The organization of the South Carolina troops with which W.P. DuBose fought at the Second Battle of Manassas, was as follows:[25]

## ARMY OF NORTHERN VIRGINIA

General Robert E. Lee, Commanding

### RIGHT WING

Lieutenant-General James Longstreet

### Evans Division

Brigadier-General N. George Evans

### Evan's Brigade

Holcombe Legion, Colonel P.F. Stevens

17th South Carolina, Col. J.H. Means

18th South Carolina, Col. J.M. Gadberry

22nd South Carolina

23rd South Carolina, Col. H.L. Benbow

Holcombe Legion, Major F.G. Palmer

TABLE 2. ORGANIZATION OF SOUTH CAROLINA TROOPS, SECOND MANASSAS

On Saturday, August 30, the Holcombe Legion fought in the Second Battle of Manassas. The approximate location of DuBose and the Holcombe Legion during the battle is shown in Figure 3. DuBose gives an excellent close-up description of their actions and the disastrous results to the Legion that day:

> We formed in line of battle, Longstreet's Corps . . . We lay under arms waiting for the battle to begin. I was sent back to see about and hurry up the wagons from the rear. As I returned, having met them and given orders, I heard cannonading begin on the field of battle. I put spurs to my horse and came as rapidly as I could upon a scene which I can never forget. On the midnight previous a battery had

arrived along the turnpike, and, not knowing exactly, not having received orders as to its station, turned aside near us on the other side of the turn-pike and had taken up a position by mere chance, which turned out to be very fortunate. It was commanded by Stephen D. Lee, afterwards General. At dawn Lee noticed the advantageous site which he had accidentally occupied and sent to request that he be allowed to remain there and hold it, which he did. As I rode back rapidly, a powerful column of enemy were advancing on that very point. It was just about the point of junction between the two corps, Longstreet's and Jackson's, which had also come up very late and occupied the position beyond. As I rode up, I just heard, boom, boom, boom, boom, boom, boom, which excited me to such a pitch, that I dashed on. Just as I got there the Yankee column had been arrested by this Battery mainly, and was wavering. As the shells were poured into them, the column dissolved and the Confederates dashed forward, hats waving in a perfect jubilation of victory . . . The excitement had scarcely subsided when the order came for a general advance along the whole line. Our Brigade was commanded at this time by Colonel Stevens and Major Palmer. Immediately in front of us and a little to the left was Hood's Brigade, and I was sent to interview General Hood and to tell him from Colonel Stevens that our brigade would keep in connection with his own. The advance began. There was between us and the very extensive battle field of Manassas a belt of rather thick woods. As we passed through this, the enemies' artillery began to play upon us, and, as we emerged into the open field, we found ourselves in a perfect focus of firing from all sides. Major Palmer and I were the only ones mounted. He called to me, "Get down!" We dismounted and the men all lay down until the heat of the fire should pass over. A few minutes later we arose to advance further to the enemy and in less time than it takes for me to tell it our whole brigade was decimated. It was said that two-thirds indeed of the men were killed or wounded. How I managed to pass through that rain of bullets I don't know, but when I emerged there was not more than a dozen, if so many, to go forward with me. The command as a whole had been annihilated. At the same time on the whole line the Confederates were victorious and so, immediately before us, the retreat began . . . I passed over the ground where one of the other brigades had fought and seeing a flag lying by the side of a dead man, I picked it up. We followed on the retreating enemy. Suddenly they halted and turned and seeing only a few individuals following them and firing at them, they proceeded to return the fire. The few men that were with me were a little to the left and were shielded somewhat from sight by some stray pine saplings. It so happened that I was the only one visible to them at that moment, standing with the flag in my hands. I had the pleasure of seeing rifles deliberately aimed at me. At the charge I fell purposely and the flag was hit and not me. I then rose and turned to run to the left. At that moment a minie ball hit me, tearing my clothes and the flesh off my back and just scraping my backbone. The enemy resumed their retreat and I was left standing there–paralyzed . . . After a little while, though, I discovered that at any rate my back was not broken and that I wasn't disabled, so I slowly made my way off the field, passing through ranks of wounded and slain men. It was an awful experience . . . The Holcombe Legion was practically destroyed as a regiment; when we gathered up the remains there were about a hundred men. I was commanded to reorganize it and to do the best possible with it in the campaign to follow. I organized the men into three companies and had hardly enough officers to man them. The victory was a great one; but it was a bloody one, one of the bloodiest of the war.[7]

### Manassas–Who Won? Southern Vs Northern Views

Colonel Stevens' official report contained in Scott gives more of an overview than did DuBose. Following are parts of Stevens' report, written near Winchester, on October 13th, six weeks after the battle: "On August 29, after a fatiguing day's march, my regiment, with the rest of the brigade, was put in line of battle in support of General Hood's brigade. The line was scarcely formed when the order was given, 'Forward.' Sleeping upon our arms that night, we were further withdrawn just before day to near the position from which we had advanced the night before. Later in the day we were again placed in battle order at this same point . . . in support of Hood's brigade . . . The enemy's fire now became very annoying, and on reaching the edge of the wood it was very severe . . . The Holcombe Legion was still in the wood . . . on the extreme right I found the line halted and staggering under the murderous fire of grape, canister and musketry which was pouring upon it . . . we charged the battery on the hill. The enemy slowly retired and left this entire portion of the field in our hands... After the capture of the battery, I can say nothing more of the brigade, I had lost it . . . all of my best officers were either killed or wounded, so that subsequent to the engagement, I had to put the Legion under command of my adjutant, Lieut. W.P. DuBose, for want of a proper officer of the line."[13]

Evans reports in the flowery language of the time the South Carolinians' part in the charge discussed by DuBose, as follows: "Over the space indicated, the South Carolinians fought with steady courage, attesting their devotion by the sacrifices of the day. In this advance fell the noble hearted Governor Means, at the head of the Seventeenth; the accomplished and gallant Glover, at the head of Hagood's First; the brave Gadberry, leading the Eighteenth; the dashing Moore, commanding the Second Rifles; the heroic Palmer, urging the Holcombe Legion to the charge, and Henry Stevens, aide to Col. P.F. Stevens, falling with five wounds."[4]

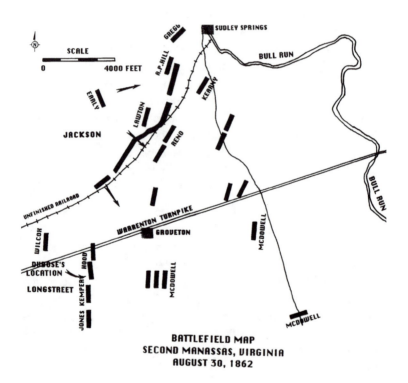

**BATTLEFIELD MAP**
**SECOND MANASSAS, VIRGINIA**
**AUGUST 30, 1862**

Information from Official Atlas of the Civil War,
and Kennedy, 1990

Figure 3

Colonel Wm. T. Wofford reported the fighting of the Holcombe Legion on the 30th, "At this battery I had no support except a mere fragment of a regiment (supposed to be the Holcombe Legion), which fought with much spirit and gallantry." [10]

Following Second Manassas on August 30, the Richmond correspondent of the *Charleston Mercury* newspaper enthusiastically and with nationalistic prejudice reported the results of the battle and the valor shown by the Southern troops involved, in particular the South Carolinians. He also listed the South Carolina officers killed and wounded during that battle.

On September 5, 1862 the *Charleston Mercury* carried this report of the battle: "The Second Battle of Manassas has been fought on precisely the same spot as that of the 21st July, 1861, with the difference that our forces occupied many of the positions which were held by the enemy at that time, and that the enemy fought upon the ground that had been held by us . . . The fight was fiercely contested until after dark, when the Yankees gave way and were driven in disorder for a distance of three miles . . . The loss of the enemy exceeds that of the Confederates in the ratio of five to one. Their dead literally cover the field. Our men captured a number of batteries, numerous regimental colors, thousands of prisoners, and from six to ten thousand stand of arms. We might have taken more of the last; but the men could not be burdened with them . . . Colonels Means, Marshall and Gadberry, of South Carolina, are killed. Colonels Benbow, Moore and McGowan, of the same State, are wounded."

The resulting action and position of the armies following the first day of the battle was confusing: apparently an easily understandable general or decisive plan of action was lacking. According to Pollard, the Northern army had no plan of attack so, the victory of the day was clearly with the Southerners. "The magnificent army swept the enemy before them, pausing only to drive them from each successive position. It was the most sublime spectacle that was ever witnessed on a battlefield. As far as the eye could range, a line of bayonets glittered in the sun. Now it could be observed passing through open fields. Again it would disappear in the woods. A brief pause would ensue, followed by the clatter of artillery riding to the front, and the awful roar of the guns. Then a shout would proclaim that the enemy was again in retreat, and the advance swept on, its bayonets catching now and then the light of the sun, while sheets of artillery fire blazed through clouds of smoke and dust. The ground which the men traversed was in many places red with blood. In wood and field, across creeks and brooks, the roar of battle continued, and long lines of smoke curling over treetops wafted away on the evening breeze. Lines of ambulances and stretchers followed the grand advance as it swept on its deliberate work of destruction, leaving scenes of carnage in its rear. Groans and deathcries arose on every hand, mingling with the distant roar and rush of battle. Still the advance was relentless. As the masses of fugitives were driven across Bull Run, many were literally dragged and crushed under the water, the crowds of frenzied men pressing and trampling upon each other in the stream. The wounded and dying of both armies lined the banks. Some, in the endeavor to drink, had tumbled in, and from weakness unable to extricate themselves, had been drowned; others in the water clung to branches, and thus sustained themselves for a little while, then were seen to let go their hold and disappear. The meadows were trodden down, wet and bloody. Hundreds of bodies had been ridden over and crushed by artillery or cavalry. In front was the brilliant spectacle of a valorous army in steady, relentless pursuit: in the rear was the ground, torn, scarred, bloody, piled with heaps of dead and dying, as monuments of war's horrors. We had driven the enemy up hill and down, a distance of two and a half miles, strewing this great space with his dead, captured thirty pieces of artillery, and some six or eight thousand stand of arms. Seven thousand prisoners were paroled on the field of battle. For want of transportation valuable stores had to be destroyed as captured, while the enemy at their various depots are reported to have burned many millions of property in their retreat." [26]

At the end of the long day of fighting, over the dark fields and valleys and in the woods behind the corpse-strewn and bloody banks of Bull Run Creek, the groans and cries of the wounded for water were distressing to the living who were unable to go safely between the lines to help them. General Stonewall Jackson's medical director, while reporting the day's extremely heavy casualties to his chief, said: "General, this day has been won by nothing but stark and stern fighting." Stonewall Jackson, who became a devoutly religious man during the war, shook his head. "No," he said. "It has been won by nothing but the blessing and protection of Providence."

The Northern interpretation of the final outcome of Second Manassas was somewhat different. The commanders were interested in justification for their actions, and the press correspondents, like the Southern journalists, were trying to avoid alarming the folks at home and to influence more support for the war effort. According to Union Major-General John Pope, at the end of the first day of battle "When the battle ceased on the 29th of August, we were in possession of the field on our right, and occupied on our left the position held early in the day, and had every right to claim a decided success. What that success might have been, if a corps of twelve thousand men who had not been in battle that day had been thrown against Longstreet's right while engaged in the severe fight that afternoon, I need not indicate. To say that General Porter's non-action during that whole day was wholly unexpected and disappointing, and that it provoked severe comment on all hands, is to state the facts mildly."[13]

Pope's additional comments following the close of the battle  on August 30-31 are equally interesting, particularly when you have just read the version of the correspondent to the *Charleston Mercury*: "Not withstanding the disadvantages under which we labored, our troops held their ground with the utmost firmness and obstinacy. The loss on both sides was heavy. By dark our left had been forced back half or three-fourths of a mile, but still remained firm and unbroken and still held the Warrenton pike on our rear, while our right was also driven back equally far, but in good order and without confusion . . . At no time during the 29th, 30th, or 31st of August was the road between Bristoe and Centreville interrupted by the enemy. The orders will show conclusively that every arrangement was made in the minutest detail for the security of our wagon train and supplies; and General Bank's subsequent report to me is positive that none of the wagons or mules were lost. I mention this matter merely to answer the wholly unfounded statements made at the time, and repeated often since, of our loss of wagons, mules, and supplies."[13]

What was the true situation following the conclusion of Second Manassas? Most seem to believe it was a Southern victory, but reading the slanted reports of the battle, it is difficult to tell. The truth of the situation probably lies somewhere between the self-defensive posture of General Pope, who was removed from command of the Union Army soon after this battle (but the victors in a war get the privilege of writing the history of the struggle) and the patriotic writings of the Charleston, South Carolina *Mercury* newspaper, which was attempting to bolster the home-folk's emotions and to assure that adherence to the cause would result in additional support, in the form of recruits, food, horses, and additional supplies necessary for war.

### What Happens When People Shoot at You?

What thoughts went through the heads of individual soldiers during major battles of the Civil War such as Second Manassas? According to a South Carolina participant defending his breastworks during the Battle of Manassas: "A battle is entered into mostly in as good order and with close a drill front as the nature of the ground will permit, but at the first 'pop! pop!' of the rifles there comes a loosening of the ranks, a freeing of selves from the impediment of contact, and every man goes to fighting on his own hook; firing as, and when he likes, and reloading as fast as he fires. Each soldier takes shelter wherever he can find it, so he does not get too far away from his company, and his officers will call his attention to this should he move too far. He may stand up, he may kneel down, he may lie down, and it is all right–though mostly the men keep standing except when silent under fire, then they lie down." [18]

## South Mountain (Boonsboro)- September 14, 1862

DuBose's travels from the Battle of Second Manassas to the time of his release from prison are shown in Figure 4. After the Seven Days and Jackson's victories in the Shenandoah Valley, there was a loud clamoring in the South for a full-scale invasion of the North and a transferal of destruction to northern lands. The Union armies seemed to be leaderless and the Southern armies and leaders appeared invincible. After Second Manassas, Southern General, James Longstreet, stated that

> When the Second Bull Run campaign closed, we had the most brilliant prospects the Confederates ever had. We then possessed an army which, had it been kept together, the Federals would never had dared attack. With such a splendid victory behind us, and such bright prospects ahead, the question arose as to whether we should go into Maryland. [20]

### Invasion of the North–The Lost Orders

Following the successful Second Manassas campaign, General Robert E. Lee agreed that the military and political interests of the South might be served by an invasion and taking of war to the cities, farms, and fields of the North. In Frederick on September 9, following the Second Battle of Manassas, General Lee believed that he was safe from Union pursuit for a while. Crossing the Potomac River as he headed north early in September, he divided his force of 45,000 men. He dispatched forces of Major General Stonewall Jackson to take Harper's Ferry, guarded only by a small Federal detachment. Taking this arsenal would help keep open lines of supply and transportation routes south. After Lee sent Jackson to Harper's Ferry, he sent Major General D.H. Hill to protect artillery trains and Major General James Longstreet to Boonsboro Gap (northwest) and the other gaps across South Mountain, located west of Frederick. Lee continued north.

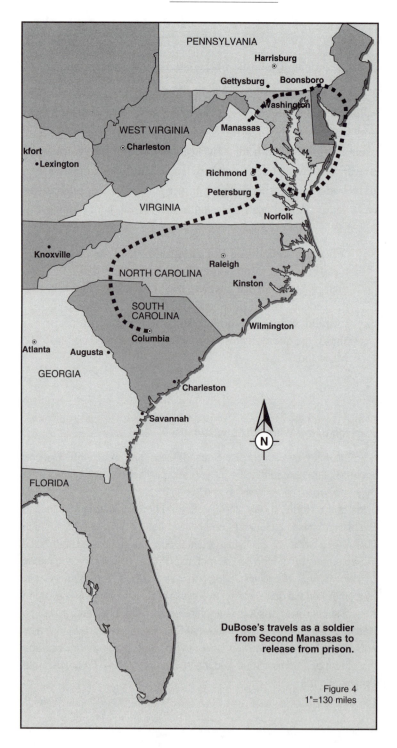

DuBose's travels as a soldier
from Second Manassas to
release from prison.

Figure 4
1"=130 miles

McClellan, just reinstated as commander of the Union forces, marched to cut Lee off. McClellan's statement concerning the move that resulted in the Battle of South Mountain was as follows: "While at Frederick, on the 13th, I obtained reliable information (writer's note–the 'lost order') of the movements and intentions of the enemy, which made it clear that it was necessary to force the passage of the South Mountain range and gain possession of Boonsborough and Rohrersville before any relief could be afforded to Harper's Ferry." [13] This account by McClellan of the splitting and placing of Lee's army is somewhat contrary to what General Longstreet remembered. General Longstreet said that, "General Lee so far changed the wording of his order as to require me to halt at Boonsboro' with General D.H. Hill; Jackson being ordered to Harper's Ferry via Bolivar Heights, on the south side; McLaws by the Maryland Heights on the north, and Walker, via Loudon Heights, from the southeast. This was afterward changed, and I was sent on to Hagerstown, leaving D.H. Hill alone at South Mountain." [19]

General Lee counted on General McClellan to move with his customary caution and McClellan did not disappoint him. He did not arrive in Frederick until four days after Lee's departure. On the morning of his arrival, a pair of soldiers from the 27th Indiana found something amazing in a recently vacated Confederate campground: two cigars, wrapped in a sheet of paper by Southern General D. Harvey Hill (brother-in-law of Stonewall Jackson). Upon inspection, the paper was found to be a copy of Lee's complete orders to split his army. One soldier smoked a cigar. The other rewrapped the other cigar with the orders and carried them to his commanding officer who carried them up the chain of command. McClellan delightedly wired President Lincoln, "I have all the plans of the rebels and will catch them in their own trap if my men are equal to the emergency. Will send you trophies. Here is a paper with which if I cannot whip Bobby Lee I will be willing to go home." [13]

The mysterious paper was Lee's Secret Order Number 191, many times called the 'lost order.' According to John Bloss of the 27th Indiana, who is given credit for finding the cigars and dispatch, the order told not only Lee's position but also his intent. Lee proposed in this 'lost order' to divide his army on the tenth. In fact, by the time the lost order was found (the 13th), the army was split into five divisions. Three of these divisions were far away attempting to capture Harper's Ferry. McClellan's army was concentrated and could strike either part of Lee's army and defeat the Confederates under the "divide and conquer" theory.

Much of McClellan's army proceeded through the gaps of Turner's Mountain and toward Hill's Division of Lee's army. The division, with 8,000 men dug in at the three gaps on South Mountain west of Boonsboro, was to face McClellan's army of some 87,000 men. Figures 5 and 6 are maps of the battlefield at South Mountain, showing DuBose and the Holcombe Legion's position. With this overwhelming force, McClellan should have been able to push through the South Mountain gaps and snare Lee's scattered army before it could reunite. McClellan set up his battle plans: "The left, therefore, was ordered to move through Jefferson to the South Mountains, at Crampton's Pass, in front of Burkittsville, while the center and right moved upon the main or Turner's Pass, in front of Middletown. During these movements I had not imposed long marches on the columns. The absolute necessity of refitting and giving some little rest to troops worn down by previous long-continued marching and severe fighting, together with the uncertainty as to the actual position, strength, and intentions of the enemy, rendered it incumbent upon me to move slowly and cautiously . . . " McClellan set up his troops to drive the enemy from the heights at Turner's Pass, most prominent of the Gaps, and to take Crampton's Pass. Success of this plan would flank the Southerners and eliminate any relief they might give to Harper's Ferry. [13]

William DuBose says that following Second Manassas, General Lee lost no time in pressing his success. He followed the retreating Federals a short distance toward Washington, turned up the Potomac as far as Leesburg into Loudon County, and then crossed into Maryland. [7]

DuBose, newly placed in command, talked years later about the forced march under near-impossible conditions:

> The next day we were off for Maryland, and crossed the Potomac near Leesburg. After this we saw no more of our wagons for some time. To pass by minor inconveniences, such as to me the want of a change of clothing after the plight in which the late battle had left me in that respect, we were without cooking utensils and were in great perplexity what to do with the little provisions we had. There was much recourse had to green apples and corn, which, as far as our brigade was concerned, was always religiously bought and paid for. Orders against plundering were rigidly enforced. In this connection I cannot help recalling a characteristic little incident of Gen. Hood, whose brigade was in our division. The roads were lined with orchards, and it was no easy matter to keep stragglers out of these orchards. Each succeeding command would send a guard to expel the stragglers of its predecessors at the point of the bayonet, only to be followed by its own stragglers, to be expelled in turn by the guard of the next command. Ge. Hood was riding lazily and sleepily at the head of his famous brigade, on one of these occasions, when something aroused him to the state of affairs. It would have been in order for him to send a guard to clear the orchard; instead of which, however, he simply lifted himself in his saddle and, turning to his men, said: 'Rock 'em, boys, rock 'em.' In a moment a cloud of stones darkened the air of the orchard, and the stragglers got out of it more quickly and in a more damaged condition than under the previous regimen of bayonets. [7]

The battered remnants of the Holcombe Legion entered Leesburg after dark. The sixteen-mile forced march to South Mountain was a courageous and difficult one: the Holcombe Legion had lost two-thirds of its men, had no doctors, medicine, or food, and DuBose himself had the painful back wound, as yet undressed. Somehow they stumbled to Boonsboro Gap. That DuBose, a Lieutenant, was still in charge of the Legion, is a highly unusual circumstance, indicating how badly the unit had been shot up in the battle.

The next morning the Legion crossed the Potomac and began the Maryland campaign. DuBose gives details about the remainder of the march through Maryland on their way to Boonsboro and the Battle of South Mountain. They arrived in Frederick City, where the Holcombe Legion was showing signs of weariness and illness. Because the Legion had no doctor and no medicine, DuBose went into town and bought a half-dozen very small bottles of pain killer. DuBose said of this:

> This kind of fare was not conducive to the physical efficiency of the troops. Not only had the cooking utensils, but the surgeons had been left behind, with their hands more than full on the bloody field of Manassas. My men soon began to fall sick and I was compelled to enter for the only time of my life upon the practice of medicine. Riding through a little village I stopped my horse at the drug store and tried to lay in a supply of drugs. There was nothing on hand but some small phials of pain killer with which I filled my pockets and began my practice. But my pain killer did not materially mend matters. We marched through Frederick City and by Boonsboro' Gap to Hagerstown, where we rested for a few days. Here my medical difficulties culminated. The first of the surgeons rejoined us here and was quietly summoned from his own regiment to my aid. We made the rounds of the sick together, and as tongue after tongue was exposed for our

scrutiny he lectured me on the nature of the typhoid symptoms which were beginning to appear. When the last tongue was examined he bowed himself politely away and left me where he had found me. In fact there was nothing to be done without medicines.[7]

The regiment had a few days respite in Hagerstown, during which DuBose was proud to report that he had the opportunity of a bath in a mountain stream and had a change of clothes. On the second or third morning in Hagerstown, they were hastily put under arms and hurried back to Boonsboro Gap.

The march back to Boonsboro Gap was a tough one on the men who were still suffering from the Second Battle of Manassas. DuBose says of the start of this battle:

> It was just in this condition that the order found us on the morning of September 14, to march immediately back to the pass or Gap of South Mountain at Boonsboro'. We did so and arrived there early in the afternoon barely in time to meet the enemy who were in the act of seizing the Gap. We were at once ordered up the height overlooking the Pass on the north. The march had been a hard one, and the men were many of them so weak and exhausted that they could scarcely climb the mountain. One poor fellow I distinctly remember. He was the one about whom I had a day or two before received my most clinical lecture upon the typhoid symptoms. He had marched manfully all the morning, but in this ascent he fell out of ranks and declared himself unable to go further. I told him we were all sick and could not spare a single man, and getting behind him I pushed him to the top. He never came down; a few minutes later he was shot in his tracks. [7]

According to DuBose, the object was to stop or slow McClellan's army in their passage across South Mountain, so General Lee could unite his army to meet them (a reference to the forthcoming Battle of Antietam).

The Holcombe Legion was immediately sent to the top of a height on the northern side. It was a steep climb and they arrived at a flat plateau bounded on the east by a line of rocky cliffs. The Northern battle reports described the ground occupied by the Legion as being of the most difficult character. The hillside was very steep and rocky and obstructed by stone walls and timber. [13]

The Holcombe Legion was deployed as skirmishers in front of the line formed behind the cliffs. DuBose says, "We had barely got into position when the enemy's heavy and overlapping line appeared slowly climbing up. It was only a question of time, a matter of *retarding* (emphasis added by DuBose) their progress, and by dark we had been forced back into the gap below. But it was too late for the enemy to make any advance that night." [7] DuBose, in his letters to the *Charleston Weekly News*, October 4, 1882, analyzed the relative positions in this deadly game of "King of the Mountain" as follows:

> In an attack of this sort the advantage is all on the side of those below. Even on level ground troops cannot be prevented from firing too high, and this tendency is indefinitely increased when the firing is down a steep slope. In Bate's History of the Pennsylvania Volunteers I have read a separate and independent sketch of each of the dozen or so Pennsylvania regiments engaged at this point, and each of them remarks upon the fact that, while in some instances the Federal flags were torn to pieces by Confederate bullets, comparatively few men were struck. On the contrary, men firing up hill do so to the best effort.

DuBose, when discussing this battle, describes the relative merits of the "Rebel Yell" versus the "Yankee Hurrah":

> I had on this occasion the best opportunity of comparing at short distances the battle cries of Federals and Confederates. The former as they ascended broke out occasionally into their regular 'Hip, hip, hurrah.' Confederate troops never stopped upon the order of their shouting, but shouted with a yell peculiarly their own.

Either was bad enough with the accompaniment of minie balls about one's ears, but in itself the yell was a more terrible thing than the ordered cheer. [7]

General Lee posted General D. H. Lee's Division in and around the gaps, on the opposite side and summit, with instructions to hold the positions. All movements were to begin the following morning, and a convergence of the divided divisions was scheduled for the 12th of September. After this, the other three divisions would rejoin Hill's Corps at the town of Boonsboro to continue Lee's campaign to the north through Maryland and into Pennsylvania. No part of the original plan was to fight a pitched battle here. By the 13th, Lee was aware that McClellan had possession of the "lost order," and ordered his troops to block the passes through South Mountain.

Figures five and six provide information on the layout of the land at South Mountain. Figure five shows the entire area and Figure six the close-up details of the area in which DuBose and the Holcombe Legion fought.

Turner's Pass, defended in part by W.P. DuBose and his fellow South Carolinians, was sometimes known as Boonsboro Gap and is a continuation over the broad back of the mountain of the (then) national turnpike. The road was winding, narrow, rocky, and rugged, with either a deep ravine on one side and the steep sides of the mountain on the other, or, the road itself was a huge channel cut through solid rock. Near the crest of the mountain were two or three houses overlooking the adjacent beautiful valleys, but the face of the mountain showed no other evidence of man.

Armed with Lee's orders, General McClellan decided to descend upon Boonsboro, where the nearest part of Lee's divided army was located, overwhelm it, and then turn on the rest of the army and destroy it bit by bit. However, he likely did not accept the lost order as completely accurate, at least in respect to the strength of Longstreet and Hill at Boonsboro Gap and the two southern gaps through South Mountain, or the extremely strong defensive topographic position of the dug-in Rebels. Once again, McClellan was slow and cautious. The Union troops could have approached the town of Boonsboro through three gaps: Crampton's Gap is southernmost, Fox Gap is the center, and Boonsboro Gap (known on topographic maps of today as Turner's Gap) is the northern gap at which DuBose fought.

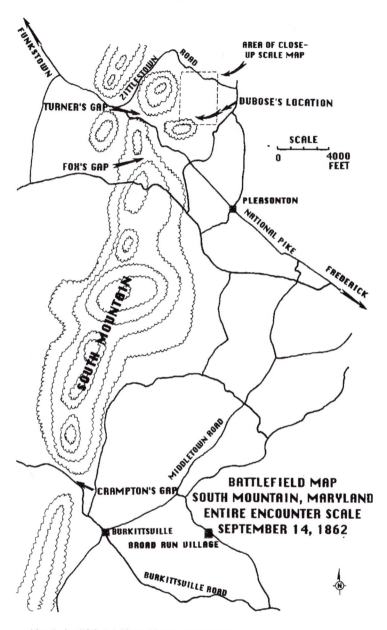

FUNKSTOWN

ZITTLESTOWN ROAD

TURNER'S GAP

FOX'S GAP

AREA OF CLOSE-UP SCALE MAP

DUBOSE'S LOCATION

SCALE

0        4000 FEET

PLEASONTON

NATIONAL PIKE

FREDERICK

SOUTH MOUNTAIN

MIDDLETOWN ROAD

CRAMPTON'S GAP

BURKITTSVILLE

BROAD RUN VILLAGE

BURKITTSVILLE ROAD

BATTLEFIELD MAP
SOUTH MOUNTAIN, MARYLAND
ENTIRE ENCOUNTER SCALE
SEPTEMBER 14, 1862

N

Information from U.S. Geological Survey; Official Atlas of the Civil War; Priest, 1992

Figure 5

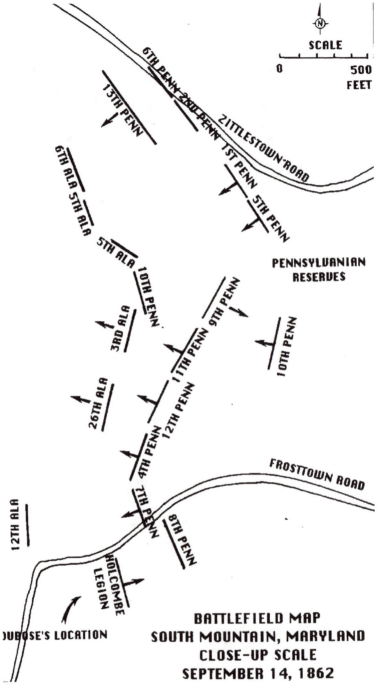

SCALE

0    500
FEET

13TH PENN

6TH PENN 2ND PENN 1ST PENN

ZITTLESTOWN ROAD

5TH PENN

6TH ALA 5TH ALA

5TH ALA

10TH PENN

PENNSYLVANIAN
RESERVES

3RD ALA

11TH PENN 9TH PENN

10TH PENN

26TH ALA

12TH PENN

4TH PENN

FROSTTOWN ROAD

12TH ALA

7TH PENN

8TH PENN

HOLCOMBE LEGION

)UBOSE'S LOCATION

**BATTLEFIELD MAP
SOUTH MOUNTAIN, MARYLAND
CLOSE-UP SCALE
SEPTEMBER 14, 1862**

Figure 6

Information from U.S. Geological Survey; Official Atlas of the Civil War;
Priest, 1992

Turner's Gap is about six miles north of Crampton's Gap, as the crow flies, but the terrain is a practically unbroken range of rugged, heavily timbered mountains. Attack or defense of each gap or pass was isolated from the others. The fighting was going on at each place on the same day, all day at Turner's Gap and in the afternoon at Cramptons Gap. The fighting at Turner's Gap was on a larger scale, took longer, and was more costly to both sides. The whole affair consisted of sharp skirmishing in and out of the thickly wooded areas and consisted of many small battles rather than one large, connected battle. The writers of the many reports of the battle(s) that occurred on that day were not always clear as to the name of the gap at which their particular part of the battle was fought. Their writing makes clear, however, that all three gaps were attacked and defended on that day, as the Union troops attempted to clear the roads across the mountain to Boonsboro.

Before sunrise on September 14th, General Hill rode to the top of South Mountain to view the front. He made sure all advanced troops were dug in at the top. As General Hill rode near Fox's Gap he heard the noise of enemy troops working their way toward him. As the artillery opened fire, he hurried back and sent General Samuel Garland's brigade to meet the Northern forces. The battle commenced soon after daylight. The two Southern batteries located on the summit of the mountain answered the cannonfire from the Union forces located at the foot of the mountain. Under cover of the cannonfire, two or three hours later, skirmishers became engaged, followed by the main bodies. Establishing a regular line of battle, as was standard operating procedure by both armies, was impossible because the steepness and ruggedness of the terrain limited the battle theater.

### One Man's View of the Battle of South Mountain and of Journalistic Honesty

A Confederate soldier, George M. Neese, fought in the defense of one of the gaps through South Mountain and recorded his thoughts in a diary. He thought that McClellan could have accomplished a quick victory if he had fully believed the lost dispatch, stating the number of men he was facing. Even if in possession of data like the Lost Orders, McClellan habitually overestimated the size of the opposing force. Neese becomes extremely sarcastic when he predicts the likely northern newspapers' reporting at the conclusion of the battle. Following are excerpts from Neese's diary: "September 14, 1862. Early dawn found us on top of South Mountain, looking over the beautiful Middletown Valley. But the booming of Yankee cannon came rolling across from the Catoctin Hills, announcing that the Yankee hosts were advancing. There are three principal gaps in South Mountain through which roads pass. We were at Crampton's Gap, which is the southernmost of the three. We had only three companies of infantry, one brigade of cavalry, and six pieces of artillery to defend the gap against two, perhaps three, divisions of Yankee infantry, with accompanying artillery and a big bunch of cavalry. The whole country seemed to be full of bluecoats. They were so numerous that it looked as if they were creeping up out of the ground- and what would or could our little force of some three or four hundred available men standing half-way up a brushy, stony mountainside do with such a mighty host. We kept up the fight until nearly night; but late in the evening the enemy forced the pass by flanking and fighting, with overwhelming numbers, and compelled our little force to retire. To observe the caution with which the Yankees, with their vastly superior numbers, approached the mountain put one in mind of a lion, king of the forest, making exceedingly careful preparations to spring on a plucky little mouse. For we had only about three hundred men actually engaged, and they were mostly cavalry, which is of very little use in defending a mountain pass. As usual, correspondents of Northern newspapers will say that a little band of heroic Union patriots gallantly cleaned out Crampton's Gap, defended by an overwhelming force of Rebels strongly posted and standing so thick that they had to crawl over each other to get away. [27]

In the afternoon General Hood arrived with two brigades of infantry; this reinforcement braced the Confederate front and the South held out until nightfall. The cessation of firing later in the day left the respective forces, with a few exceptions, in nearly the same relative positions as at the beginning of the battle. The overall goal of the Confederates to hold the gaps and to delay McClellan was realized, but neither Northern nor Southern forces gained much new territory. Although costly to Lee (Southern losses were 2,700 men compared with McClellan's 1,800), the defense of Boonsboro Gap and the other South Mountain gaps delayed the overall Northern advance. McClellan had lost his chance to save the garrison of Harper's Ferry and to take Lee's divided Army to avoid the regrouping of the forces.

By nightfall, the Union advance had been slowed at Fox's and Turner's gaps but had smashed through at Crampton's Gap. Once again through timid leadership, the Union forces failed to capitalize on opportunities and failed to save Harper's Ferry. Lee, rather than concede the fact that the Union army would successfully cross South Mountain the next day, decided to concentrate the whole army at Sharpsburg and offer battle.

The Holcombe Legion had not turned in its usual heroic fight throughout the day: they apparently turned tail and ran when faced with the overwhelming forces of Union troops. Colonel Stevens, in his official battle report, described the disastrous afternoon's activities as follows:

> Here I found the Twenty-third and Twenty-second driven back, but rallied under Captains Durham and (M.) Hilton, respectively. Very soon the Eighteenth retired also, and from that time the fight was a retreating one until the enemy occupied the mountain and we were driven from it. General Rodes was at the same time forced back on my left. Captain Durham and Adjutant DuBose were conspicuous in their efforts to stay the retreat, but I am con-

strained to say that after falling back I cannot commend the behavior of the men. Some two or three bravely faced the foe, but a general lack of discipline and disregard for officers prevailed all around me . . . The brigade having reassembled on the turnpike, I threw out the legion on picket deployed along the skirt of woods on the mountain we had just left . . . [13]

After the fierce battle, as dark was settling in, DuBose and his exhausted men sank in their tracks on the turnpike for a moment's rest. According to DuBose, "It was only for a moment, just long enough to feel the utter exhaustion that followed, a day every moment of which had been spent in marching, climbing, fighting, and ending at last in defeat." [7] As Lee had used DuBose and his depleted regiment as the picket line of that Corps of the Army, DuBose was quickly roused with an order to strike a picket line on the heights, which he did although according to DuBose, "This was no easy task on a dark night in the primeval forest." [6] DuBose and his men then collapsed once again in an effort to find rest. He was roused again and received an order to take his command back up the mountain to the scene of the battle to determine if General Lee was correct and the enemy had left. DuBose was to carry his reconnaissance as far as the battlefield of the day.

At 11:00 P.M., DuBose and a few of his men began climbing the heights. He stationed the men a few tens of feet apart as they ascended and then DuBose went up the last of the mountain alone. He describes the climb up the mountain as, " . . . a heavy and, unavoidably, a noisy as well as dangerous climb." [6] He arrived on top of the plateau and did not notice any enemy soldiers. He crossed the battlefield and searched in the dark for the bodies of his men that had been left there that day, apparently to mark the spots and arrange for a burial detail the next day.

After completing the difficult walk, DuBose decided to make a detour on the way back down to examine the other side of the plateau. He was feeling pretty proud of himself and was framing his report to General Lee in his mind when he suddenly heard, "Halt!" He could see the outline of one man under the trees and, hoping that it was one of his own men, proceeded carefully to reach beneath his cloak for the pistol hidden there. The figure spoke again, "Halt and give the countersign." DuBose realized that he was in trouble and reached for the pistol, which accidentally discharged, hitting no one. The man jumped on DuBose, and they struggled on the ground as the man yelled at the top of his voice.

The guard's yells and the pistol awakened a host of sleeping men, who overpowered DuBose and took him prisoner, after he had unsuccessfully tried to confuse them by shouting "Charge!" over and over again. DuBose was in real trouble; the borrowed cloak in which he was captured was a civilian's cape and suggested the disguise of a spy. If convicted as such, he would have faced a firing squad, an inauspicious end for a man who was close to becoming a priest prior to the war. But luckily, the Yankees accepted that he was, indeed, a soldier. DuBose had been captured by Colonel Fisher of the 107th Pennsylvania Volunteers. After questioning him, the Yankees went back to sleep, leaving DuBose guarded, and he, exhausted from the past several days' activities, also fell into a deep sleep.

An interesting sideline to this story is that decades after this capture incident, a man named Daniel Cronin, who had served as a private with the 107th Pennsylvania Volunteers, came to DuBose with information regarding the capture that only the sentinel would have known. DuBose prepared an affidavit of the incident that Cronin hoped would bring him a pension from the Federal government. Apparently, Cronin's war records had been misplaced or were too sketchy to satisfy the board making decisions on the granting of pensions.

DuBose says in *Turning Points* that he occasionally received letters from Cronin and, to DuBose's utter surprise, Cronin visited him about thirty-five years after the Battle of South Mountain. DuBose says that:

> He (Cronin) suddenly appeared there (The University of the South), ill and travel-worn, having made the journey across several States to see me again before he died. He said he had come near killing me; for when I had twice almost got away, he had at last, being of twice my strength, got me down, and then, with my own pistol, was in the act of shooting, when some mysterious force had held his hand and prevented him. He made me sit down and write for him an account of our two encounters in war and in peace, and then as mysteriously made his disappearance. [6]

The following morning DuBose awoke to find two Irish guards present; the rest of the 107th Pennsylvania was gone. The mountain was abandoned except for the three men. DuBose was escorted off the mountain to a small camp, where he was placed in the charge of a officer, who, prior to the war, was a cabinetmaker from Pennsylvania. The officer came to trust DuBose, so the two of them stood and watched McClellan's army march by on their way to Sharpsburg. DuBose was absolutely amazed at the size of the army. Compared with his own Confederate experiences, he was equally amazed at how McClellan had organized and furnished such a huge and organized and well-supplied army in a short time. As command after command of infantry and artillery marched by, DuBose's heart sank in his chest at the thought of Lee's thirty thousand ragged, hungry, and sick men awaiting this splendid army of eighty thousand (DuBose called them Lee's Miserables, a term borrowed from Victor Hugo and commonly used by the veterans of the Army of Northern Virginia when referring to themselves).

DuBose and his guard, now turned friend, stopped at a small roadside hut that was serving fresh, hot food. DuBose had a sudden loss of appetite when he realized that all he had was Confederate money, but his guard paid for the meals. DuBose was amazed at how little inflation had impacted the north, as several nickels covered the meal. DuBose had been used to spending several Confederate dollars for such a meal.

As the Federal army retired to Frederick, DuBose was transferred to a cavalry command, where he found himself to be one of a dozen captured Southern officers. They were placed together in a small room, where local Southern sympathizers brought food to the prisoners. From Frederick the prisoners were transported to Baltimore and marched through the streets in a drizzling rain. DuBose was surprised at the expressions of sympathy he noticed from the Marylanders. The prisoners were then transported by boat to the little canal that connects the Chesapeake Bay with Delaware Bay and then to Fort Delaware. On the crowded trip by boat, DuBose had to choose between sleeping in a narrow space between men or standing up for the entire night. DuBose opted for sleep and was, unfortunately, as he discovered three or four days later, infected with what he referred to as " . . . the very worst form of dirt-*live* (Note: emphasis added by DuBose) dirt." [7] In other words, he had acquired that scourge of both armies, body lice.

Following William DuBose's disappearance the evening following the Battle of South Mountain, those left behind were not certain whether he had been killed or captured. No Southerners had witnessed the capture. DuBose's cousin, Franklin Gaillard, in his *Civil War Letters*, wrote to his wife from a camp near Winchester on October 14th, 1862: "I wish we could hear something of Willie DuBose. I can not but hope he is alive. The chances are greatly in favor of his being still alive. He was fired at at night and but one shot was fired." [28]

Colonel Stevens, in his battle report, written a month later on October 13th in camp near Winchester, Virginia, was still not sure if DuBose had survived. He described the reconnaissance of DuBose and in addition provided a testimonial, as follows:

About 11 or 12 o'clock I received an order from General R.E. Lee to send a small detachment back to the ground where I had fought and ascertain whether the enemy still occupies it or had retired. This duty I entrusted to Lieutenant DuBose, then on picket. Advancing to the battle-ground, or nearly to it, the lieutenant left his men and moved on alone. In a few moments a shot was fired and a cry was heard. Falling back some 100 yards, his men waited in vain for his return to them, and two or three of the enemy having been seen, they returned to report the loss of their beloved leader. Whether that single shot proved fatal or whether he is a prisoner I know not, but in him I have lost my right arm, and the service of as noble, as pure-minded, as fearless an officer as ever battled for his country. [13]

When he arrived in Richmond following his parole some months later DuBose discovered that on the night of his capture, his men were waiting for him to return from the battlefield on the plateau and heard the shouts and the shot. They drew the conclusion that DuBose had been killed, went back down the mountain, and followed the path of the army, which had by then departed. They reported DuBose's suspected death. Colonel Stevens, commandant of the Holcombe Legion, resigned his commission and reassumed his church orders shortly after this incident. He named his new-born son after DuBose, assuming that he was dead and feeling responsible because he had sent DuBose on the mission.

The day following his arrival in Richmond to begin serving his parole, DuBose met another former Citadel man, who asked where DuBose's brother, "William" was. DuBose replied, "I am my brother William, myself." The man responded, "You aren't. He's dead." He took DuBose to a Richmond reading room to show him the newspaper article and a brief notice about DuBose written by Mr. Yeadon of Charleston, reporting DuBose's death. [7] DuBose did not record his reaction to this event in his *Reminiscences* but I would suspect that he would have contacted the newspaper to have a retraction written also sent word home so his family and friends would know he had survived the battle and the imprisonment.

At South Mountain and Sharpsburg, with no further interference by the Northern army, the Southern army rejoined forces. General Lee realized the prospect of continuing the fight at the present location was not good. Because of the combination of the great force of the enemy and their commanding position on both flanks, along with the cramped position of the Confederates, Lee decided to withdraw over the mountain to Sharpsburg. Once again McClellan was faced with all of Lee's forces, although they were fewer than McClellan's intelligence led him to believe. The result was the bloody Battle of Antietam, which McClellan fought in his usual timid manner.20 After Antietam, McClellan again failed or refused to seize the opportunity and allowed Lee to escape across the Potomac River.

DuBose could get no straight answers from his Northern guards as to how the battles of Sharpsburg or Antietam were going, but from the guards' attitudes, which worsened as the afternoon wore on, he and the other Confederate prisoners were able to surmise that the battles went the way of the Rebels. Some twenty years after the war, DuBose wrote that "For my part it seemed that Gen. Lee, in so paralyzing McClellan as to be able to cross the Potomac in peace and safety, had accomplished little less than a miracle; and still I cannot but regard Sharpsburg as one of the greatest triumphs of the war." [7]

### Lee's Miserables

History is full of reports of the condition of Lee's armies and the individual soldiers following the marches and battles during the months of August and September, 1862. Perhaps the story is best told in a portion of *Caldwell's History*, quoted by Evans: "It is difficult to describe the condition of the troops at this time, so great and various was their wretchedness. They were sunburnt, gaunt, ragged, scarcely at all specters and caricatures of their former selves. Since the beginning of August they had been almost constantly on the march, had been scorched by the sultriest sun of the year, had been drenched by the rain and the heavy dews peculiar to this latitude, had lost much night rest, had worn out their clothing and shoes, and received nothing but what they could pick up on the battlefield. They had thrown away their knapsacks and blankets, in order to travel light; had fed on half-cooked dough, often raw bacon as well as raw beef; had devoured green corn and green apples, and contracted diarrhea and dysentery of the most malignant type. They now stood, an emaciated, limping, ragged mass, whom no stranger to their gallant exploits could have believed capable of anything the least worthy. [4]

### Federal Prison- Fort Delaware

Prisons, both North and South, were one of the darkest chapters of the war. From the beginning there were problems regarding treatment of prisoners. Confederate prisoners were at first considered to be traitors to the Union and could have been subject to the death penalty. Circumstances, along with the quickly enlarging magnitude of the war, forced the Union to recognize Confederate prisoners as legitimate prisoners of war. Conditions were universally bad in both the Northern and Southern prison camps. All were overcrowded, few had adequate food, shelter, or clothing, and medical and sanitary services were virtually nonexistent.

William DuBose spent several weeks in Fort Delaware Federal Prison following his capture at South Mountain. Other books about DuBose say that he spent a substantial number of months in the prison, but his military records on microfilm at the South Carolina Archives in Columbia show that he was incarcerated in Fort Delaware for only a few weeks: he was captured on September 13, 1862, moved from Fort Delaware and sent to Aiken's Landing for parole on October 2, 1862, and received his final parole on November 10, 1862. Figure 7 shows the travels DuBose was to make during the time period between his release from prison and his movement to the Savannah/Charleston area.

Fort Delaware was considered by many to be the Northern equivalent of Andersonville. It was located on an island in the Delaware River. Much of the island was marsh or below water, held back by dikes. The flimsy wooden barracks in which the men lived were cold and damp.

Unlike most prisons, Fort Delaware housed both officers and enlisted or drafted men. DuBose described Fort Delaware as built around a large court or parade-ground. The whole length of the area

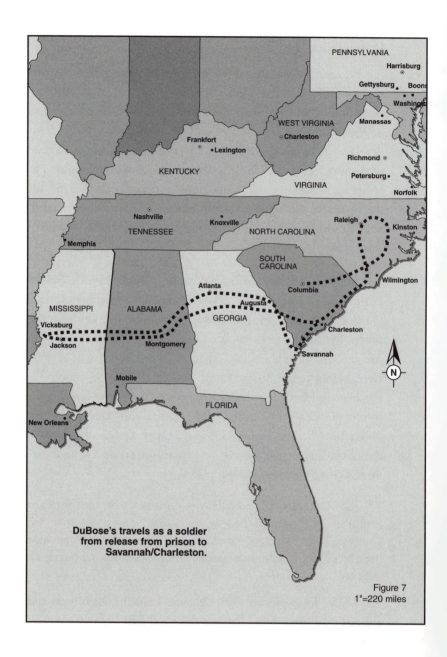

DuBose's travels as a soldier
from release from prison to
Savannah/Charleston.

Figure 7
1"=220 miles

between the interior court and the river was occupied by a long room in which the officers were imprisoned. DuBose said that there were seventy-five of his fellow officers at the time of his incarceration. All of them shared the same continuous bunk that ran the length of the room. To relieve themselves the prisoners used the windows overlooking the river. Having painfully learned from his recent experience with "live dirt," DuBose created a bunk for himself out of two shoe cartons near the windows to the inner court. I would call this a completely understandable form of elitism.

The back wound which DuBose had received at Manassas was still largely unhealed and had the appearance of the bullet having gone straight through his backbone. As DuBose took a half-bath each morning, he drew shocked attention from his fellow prisoners because of the awful appearance of the open wound.

The lack of organization or law among the prisoners resulted in mad scrambles and virtual fights whenever supplies were brought to the officers. DuBose refused to become involved in these activities and, as a result, lacked many necessities, such as shoes. During his stay at Fort Delaware, DuBose was able to keep his tiny library with him. He continued to study in solitude "the true mind and meaning of the . . . intensely human and real St. Paul." So, prisoner DuBose found a feeling of emancipation in the thoughts of his fellow prisoner, St. Paul, as he set out on a lifelong project of studying, meditating, and writing on the Epistles of Paul. Being granted permission to retain his books was a possibility only in the first few years of the war. After the North became aware of the situation at Andersonville Confederate prison camp, the conditions at Northern prison camps were tightened considerably. Dickart states that he and his fellow prisoners were carefully examined and searched, and no valuables at all were allowed. They were, however, able to keep their tobacco. [15]

During his stay at Fort Delaware, DuBose found a number of friends, particularly men he had known at the University of Virginia. He renewed an acquaintance with Dr. J.W. Tustin, who had been a minister of the Huguenot Church in Charleston. Dr. Tustin, who was conducting services in the prison as a visiting missionary, kept up with DuBose for years after the war and sent money to help mission churches with which DuBose was associated. After Tustin's death DuBose was contacted by his widow who planned to come to see DuBose at The University of the South. She died before the visit, but within a year, The University of the South was the recipient of a bequest of thirty thousand dollars from Dr. Tustin's will. [7]

After three weeks in Fort Delaware Prison, DuBose mentions persistent rumors that circulated about the possible exchange or parole of the officers in the prison. DuBose admits that at this time he "completely lost control of my philosophy or religion and spent most of my time gazing up the river to see the boat that was to take us away. After much hope deferred it actually came, and we embarked upon my first sea voyage–around to Richmond."[7] DuBose, in retrospect, said that his only "official" disagreeable experience at Fort Delaware was when he was summoned before the Commandant, as were most of the officers, and asked to give information about the Confederate Army and affairs generally. Did they answer the questions in response to the pressure exerted? I think not, as DuBose summed it up with, "An effort was made to extort this information, but in one way or another, I think we all succeeded in not contributing much to the information desired." [7]

Following his release DuBose and the other parolees arrived at Richmond, Virginia, where hunger became their largest problem. They were placed under an informal "honor system", and ordered to report from time to time to a parole camp until they could be exchanged. After weeks of waiting for the formal exchange to take place, DuBose found a way to sit out the wait at home. DuBose met with a doctor friend and relative of his, Dr. Edwin Gaillard, Chief

Surgeon of the Confederacy, who promptly gave him a sick leave and a furlough, so DuBose went home to Winnsboro, South Carolina. He was able to recuperate from his earlier wound and incarceration comfortably at home with his loved ones.

### Military Prisons–Not a Pleasant Place To Spend a War

Of thousands of Confederates who were not as fortunate as DuBose with his brief prison time, and who spent months or years in Federal prisons such as Fort Delaware, Point Lookout, Fort Warren, Johnson's Island, Elmira, or others, only a few wrote books about their experiences. One was Anthony Keiley from Petersburg, Virginia, who spent months in Point Lookout Prison. He paints a picture of an environment remarkably similar to the more publicized Northern versions of Confederate prisons such as Andersonville and Salisbury. Describing the food, Keiley says, "I never saw any one get enough of any thing to eat at Point Lookout, except the soup, and a tea spoonful of that was too much for ordinary digestion."29 Keiley goes on to describe the drinking water: "so impregnated with some mineral as to offend every nose, and induce diarrhoea (sic) in almost every alimentary canal. It colors every thing black in which it is allowed to rest, and a scum rises on the top of a vessel if it is left standing during the night, which reflects the prismatic colors as distinctly as the surface of a stagnant pool . . . There are wells outside of the pen which are not liable to these charges, the water of which is indeed perfectly pure and wholesome, so that the Yanks suffer no damage therefrom. [29]

The drinking water at Fort Delaware was equally delightful to that described by Keiley at Point Lookout, according to one rebel prisoner locked up there: "The standing rain water breeds a dense swarm of animalculae (and when the) interior sediment is stirred up . . . the whole contents become a turgid, jellified mass of waggle tails, worms, dead leaves, dead fishes and other putrescent abominations . . . The smell of it is enough to revolt the stomach . . . to say nothing of making one's throat a channel for such stuff." [30]

Prison camps, North and South, killed more men (fifty thousand) than were killed even at the bloody Battle of Gettysburg. Deaths were caused by disease, lack of food, cold, and in some cases, ill treatment from the guards. Prisoners who violated rules were sometimes hanged by their thumbs, beaten, or "bucked and gagged." Guards were quick to shoot with little or no provocation. According to Barziza, "Reward was given for crime. It was understood that a sentinel who shot a prisoner consistently with orders, should be rewarded by promotion or money."31 Confederate I.W.K. Handy, imprisoned at Fort Delaware, describes the unfortunate shooting of a Virginia colonel in 1864. The colonel was suffering from foot disease and the common scourge of the camps, diarrhea. He was shot and killed as he was returning from the privy. He was literally fastening his trousers, and was too slow to respond to a guard's challenge. Handy goes on to say, that: "The boy who shot Colonel Jones is again on guard this morning; and it is reported that he has been promoted to a corporalcy. He belongs, I think, to an Ohio regiment, is about eighteen years old, and is known as Bill Douglas."[32]

Food was in short supply; "as there was little currency . . . tobacco, rats, pickles, pork, and light bread were mediums of exchange. Five chews of tobacco would buy a rat, a rat would buy five chews of tobacco, a loaf of bread would buy a rat, a rat would buy a loaf of bread."30 The food at Fort Delaware was also scanty, at best. "How strange a thing it is to be hungry! Actually craving something to eat, and constantly thinking about it from morning to night, from day to day; for weeks and months!. . . For the past month our rations have been six, sometimes four hard crackers and 1/10 of a pound of rusty bacon (a piece the size of a hen's egg) for the twenty-four hours.   But for five days past we have not had a morsel of meat of any kind; the cooks alleging that the supply ran short and "spoiled." (For a fortnight before it ceased to be issued, the rations were so full of worms and stank so that one had to hold his nose while eating it!) But now we receive *none at all* ! Talk about Andersonville! We would gladly exchange rations with the Yankees there! The catching and eating of the huge rats which infest the island has become a common thing. It is a curious sight; grown men, whiskered and uniformed officers . . . lurking, club in hand, near one of the many breathing holes, which the long-tailed rodents have cut in the hard earth, patiently awaiting a chance to strike a blow for "fresh meat and rat soup" for dinner! They generally succeed in getting one or more rats at a sitting . . . They are eaten by fully a score of the officers, and apparently with relish.   When deviled or stewed, they resemble young squirrels *in looks.* "[29]

Fort Delaware, according to Barziza, is spoken of by all who were confined there as a perfect "Hell on Earth." The Commandant of this Northern prison was Brigadier General Albin Francisco Schoepf, a Polish emigrant, who before the war had been a lager-beer vender in St. Louis. Schoepf was unpopular with the Southern prisoners. Barziza called the prison a bed of mud and filth and said that the Southerners went bare-footed and their pants rolled up, when walking in the yard. He went on to say that "the filth and offal of the prison were mingled with the water they drank, and hundreds died of disease . . . The prisoners were half fed and almost naked . . . many have found a watery grave in their attempts to escape, rather than remain and die by piece meal." A few prisoners took the oath of allegiance to gain release, but they stated to their comrades that they did not feel bound by it. Barziza accused the Yankees of starving, ill-treating, and allowing the prisoners to suffer from the cold to force them to take the oath. [31]

## The Bridges at Kinston, North Carolina–December 14, 1862

At this stage in the war, prisoners were exchanged one-for-one, with an enemy soldier of equivalent rank. They were transported to their own side of the line and then required on their honor to wait there until the word of their exchange counterpart's arrival on his side of the line and the completion of the paperwork. After waiting for the completion of the parole in Richmond, DuBose spent a pleasant two weeks of convalescence at Winnsboro because of his medical release. DuBose's travels as a soldier from his release from prison through the campaigns at Savannah and Charleston are shown in Figure 7. After being formally exchanged he returned to the Holcombe Legion, which by that time was stationed near Wilmington, North Carolina.

Later in December the legion was sent to Goldsboro, North Carolina, where an important connection of the East Coast Railway was threatened by a Federal expedition moving up river from New Bern. To meet this threat they moved east to Kinston to defend a bridge over the river south of Kinston. The Holcombe Legion with other North and South Carolina units, was detailed to this task. Before we get into the battle, we will look at background information.

The State of North Carolina was ultimately invaded from all four compass directions and substantial fighting was conducted in the state during the four-year war. Most of the battles were relatively small, though nevertheless important in the overall strategies of the war leaders. Lee's operations in Virginia were to a large extent controlled by conditions in North Carolina.

### The "Old Mullet Line" Carried Fish, Then Made Battle Possible

Kinston, North Carolina, representatives were a part of the first North Carolina Internal Improvements Convention held in Raleigh in 1833. The delegates abandoned hope and earlier plans to make the Neuse River navigable and, instead planned construction of a railroad from the Port of Beaufort through Trenton and Kinston and on to Goldsboro. In 1852, the Atlantic and North Carolina Railroad Company, a private company, was chartered to build the railroad. One-third of the cost was to come from local stock purchases and two-thirds from the state. The construction was completed, and the first train ran between Goldsboro and Kinston on April 29, 1858. The day train was known as the "ShooFly" and the night train was called the "Cannonball." The railroad was dubbed "The Old Mullet Line" because it frequently carried fresh seafood inward from the coast. [33]

When New Bern along with much of the east coast of North Carolina fell to Union General Burnside in 1862, Kinston became the strategic center for Confederate forces in defense of the interior of the state and became a launching point for attacks aimed at regaining eastern coastal territory from the Northern invaders. From 1862 to 1865, numerous skirmishes took place and two major battles occurred in the Kinston area.

The first battle for Kinston, the one in which DuBose participated, took place in December, 1862, and was part of Union General Foster's desire to destroy the important Wilmington-Weldon railroad bridge across the Neuse in Goldsboro. The expedition was to be coordinated with the overall Union advance on Fredericksburg, Virginia. This railroad provided transportation for military supplies from Southern blockade runners from Wilmington to General Lee's army in Virginia. Figure 8 is a battlefield map showing the approximate location of DuBose and the Holcombe Legion during the 1862 battle for the bridges.

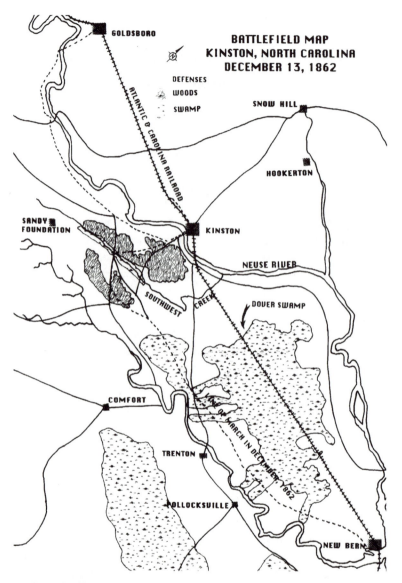

Information from Official Atlas of the Civil War; Barrett, 1963

Figure 8

The Yankee force that General Foster led forth on that bitterly cold day in December, 1862, consisted of 10,000 infantry, 40 pieces of artillery, 640 cavalry, and nine gunboats carrying 19 heavy guns.33 They left New Bern on December 11th and took the Trent Road for 14 miles until they were blocked by felled trees. They camped for the night and then left early the next morning, when it was so cold that the water reportedly froze in the men's canteens. By noon on the 12th, they reached a crossroads that led to Kinston. General Foster ordered three companies of cavalry to make themselves obvious on the Kinston Road and sent the remainder of the army toward Goldsboro.

Northern General Foster advanced as far as Southwest Creek a few miles south of Kinston. There he found the bridge destroyed and a dug-in force of Confederates led by Colonel James D. Radcliffe (North Carolina Sixty-first). The creek was deep here and could not be forded or waded, so Foster ordered the Ninth New Jersey and the Eighty-fifth Pennsylvania to swim the creek. They did so and dislodged Radcliffe's forces.

At this point Brigadier General Nathan George "Shanks" Evans arrived, took command of the Confederate forces, and ordered a retreat toward the Neuse River. Evans' command included, among others, the Holcombe Legion, commanded by Colonel P.F. Stevens.4 The Confederates then dug in about two miles from the Kinston Bridge. Evans posted his men in a strong position, taking advantage of the woods and the natural "breastworks" of the topography of the area. The right flank was protected by a deep swamp and the left by a river bend. The strength of General Evans' force at this point was about 2,014 men and included the 17th, 22nd, 23rd, and Holcombe Legion Volunteers, and Colonel Radcliffe's 61st, Major Peter Mallett's Battalion, Royce's Light Battery, and Captain S.R. Bunting and Captain J.B. Starr's artillery batteries from North Carolina. [4]

On the morning of December 14th, General Evans, with the South Carolinians, including W.P. DuBose with the Holcombe Legion and the North Carolinians on the right, awaited the attack from General Foster and his 10,640 infantry and cavalry. The attack began at 9:00 A.M., with skirmishing by the 9th New Jersey in the woods on both sides of the road. The advance was slow and steady until the firing of the dug-in Confederates caused the Yankees to stop moving and to dig in. The woods provided such good cover for the Confederates that for a while it was truly a "blind battle."

The foes were barely 75 yards apart, and the rapid firing was, according to one South Carolina soldier, " . . . a time to try the soul, the balls whizzing past and men falling around." During the battle Evans had the support of Colonel Pool's heavy artillery, located in the Neuse two miles below Kinston. A fleet of Yankee gunboats, planned to support Foster, was unable to help because low water and Colonel Pool's guns kept them from reaching Kinston.

### Official Report–Battle of Kinston

A few weeks after the battle, Confederate Major-General G.W. Smith, commander, filed his official report of the occurrences at Kinston.13 Some of these descriptions match closely with DuBose's Reminiscences. However, I present them also because they give a better "bird's eye view" of the battle, which actually was a series of four skirmishes: Southwest Creek, Kinston, White Hall and Goldsboro. Several of these particularly Kinston and Goldsboro, were so large that they approached the battle level. They all took place over five days from December 13th to the 17th.

Following are excerpts from General Smith's report: "Brigadier-General Evans, with 2,000 men, held them in check at Southwest Creek, beyond Kinston, on the 13th, and on the 14th delayed their advance for some time and succeeded in withdrawing his force with small loss to the left bank of the Neuse River at Kinston. He held them at bay until the 16th, when they advanced on the opposite side of the river and made an attach at White Hall Bridge, about 18 miles below Goldsborough, in which they were driven back by General Roberts with severe loss . . . reinforcements arrived from Petersburg and Wilmington on the 15th, one regiment of which was placed in position to cover the railroad bridge over the Neuse... On the 16th a regiment arrived from Wilmington and one from Petersburg, both of which were sent to the right bank of the river and placed under General Clingman's command to protect the two bridges... About 2 o'clock in the afternoon one bold and daring incendiary succeeded in reaching the bridge, and . . . succeeded in lighting a flame which soon destroyed the superstructure, leaving the masonry abutments and pier intact . . . It was very important for us now to save the county bridge, the only means remaining of crossing the river in this vicinity. . . The enemy were driven back from their position on the line of the railroad . . . During the night the enemy made a hurried retreat to their fortifications and gunboats . . . I regret that this grand army of invasion did not remain in the interior long enough for us to get at them." [13]

The following, taken from DuBose's *Reminiscences*, is a more ground level description of the part of the battle in which he and the Holcombe Legion participated and in which he received the most serious wound of his wartime experience:

We formed in line on the other side of the bridge from Kinston, expecting an immediate action. It was late in the afternoon and we were kept in suspense and constant expectation. I was in command of the Holcombe Legion and as morning began to approach, worn out and unnerved by the long waiting, the command was naturally in a rather demoralized condition. I believe it is acknowledged that life is at the lowest ebb at three or four o'clock in the morning. Certainly ours was that morning, when all of a sudden there was a rapid discharge of musketry in our immediate front. In a few moments our own outposts began to run in; if ever a panic might have been justified it might have been that morning at that hour. To help it and almost produce it, I received the command to fall back and take up a better position about fifty yards behind where we were in line, where the slope of the ground was more favorable to us. Such a command at that critical moment was an awful blunder. The enemy was coming on and our men had been suddenly awakened and surprised. A panic practically began, and I have never in my life had to work harder, fortunately for myself, than in taking up that new position and bringing the men up to the point of meeting the enemy. The moment, however, that they got into action, everything was instantly restored and they were as cool in possession of themselves as possible. As I walked up and down the line producing this effect, a minie ball entered my side, fired from a distance of not more than a hundred yards. Fortunately the ball had scraped a part of itself off on the slope just in front of us and then passed through a half-dozen thick folds of clothing. As it was, it touched at least two mortal spots without penetrating. I had no feeling as I was suddenly hurried away in a stretcher to the rear. As we passed over the bridge we came up to General Evans, who commanded the operations. The general stopped the stretcher and asked who it was. When he discovered, he said, 'Ah, poor fellow, poor fellow!'–and drew out a flask of whiskey. [7]

### More on the Battle of Kinston

Northern General Foster placed his artillery in a field, to the right side of the road in the direction they were moving and three-quarters of a mile in the rear of his battle line. Many of the troops were green and participating in their first battle. Some fired on their fellow Northerners, as well as having "friendly fire" dropped on them by their own artillery. After five hours of heavy firing the Union troops turned the Confederate's left flank and forced General Evans' South Carolinians to retreat across the bridge. For some unknown reason no orders were given to the center and the right, and General Evans mistakenly ordered the bridge to be fired. Unfortunately, he then opened fire upon his own Confederate right, thinking they were the enemy. He had made exactly the same "friendly fire" error as the Yankees had made earlier.

Under the agony of the friendly fire and the mounting Union pressure, the isolated Confederates gave way with what was, at first, an orderly retreat. It quickly turned into a panic as men trampled each other trying to cross the burning bridge. The Union army was close behind and captured about 400 of Evan's men who were not able to cross the river. General Evans reformed his remaining troops with the 47th North Carolina, which had just arrived, into a line on Washington Ridge two miles from Kinston. He received a message from General Foster demanding surrender. According to history, his reply was either, "Tell your General to go to Hell!", or, "Tell General Foster I will fight him here." After receipt of this message (whichever one), General Foster resumed the attack, but the Confederate troops under General Evans had fallen back to a better position at the Kennedy Home, and Foster bivouacked his army for the night in the adjoining fields.

The next morning General Foster's troops re-crossed the Neuse on the partially destroyed bridge and moved to Whitehall on River Road. Foster left behind many bitter memories for the civilians of Kinston; the Union troops looted and plundered houses and then burned the town as they departed. [33]

In summary, General Evans managed to delay the Northern advance for some time and then withdrew his forces to the left bank of the Neuse River at Kinston. He held the Yankees at bay until December 16th. The ultimate goal of the Southerners had been to protect the Atlantic and North Carolina railroad bridge over the Neuse and the county bridge about a half mile upstream; the Northerners hoped to destroy the two bridges completely. The railroad bridge was burned by the Northern troops, but they left the masonry, abutments, and pier intact.

The battle then shifted to an attempt by the Southerners to save the county bridge which was the only remaining means of crossing the river in the vicinity. The invaders also burned the superstructure of that bridge. A small victory for the defending Southern troops was that the total cost of building the two bridges was originally less than ten thousand dollars. [23] The Southern losses in the battle were not large; seventy-one killed and sixty-eight wounded. The Northern occupation of Kinston and the bridge prevented a body of about 400 Southerners from escaping. Most of them were captured, taken prisoner, and paroled; a few men succeeded in escaping higher up the river. DuBose said later of the battle, "I will only say with regard to the military operations, that the enemy did not reach their objective point and break the connections as they intended." [7] An interesting comment, considering the Northerners indeed managed to burn both bridges. Perhaps DuBose was thinking more about the railroad line, which escaped relatively unscathed.

Following the battle, General Evans mentioned DuBose in reports several times and recommended him for promotion. General Evans in his official report lauded his men: "especially the gallant conduct of Adjt. W.P. DuBose and Capt. M.G. Zeigler of the Holcombe Legion; Capt. S.A. Durham, Twenty-third South Carolina; his personal staff, and Lieutenant-Colonels Mallett and Pool, and Colonels Radcliffe and Baker of the North Carolina troops." [4] In another version of the report Evans says that: "The following officers were observed by myself as conspicuous in the battles of Saturday and Sunday: Col. P. Mallett, North Carolina Troops; Capt. Ziegler, Holcombe Legion; Adj. W.P. DuBose, wounded while leading his regiment; Capt. Durham, Twenty-third South Carolina Volunteers, wounded severely leading his regiment in action at the railroad." [13]

After this wound, the surgeons were able to probe and remove the minie ball, leaving DuBose painfully, but happily not mortally wounded. In a painful ride in an army ambulance he was taken to Goldsboro and treated. He was then taken to Raleigh to St. Mary's School, in use as a hospital. Indications were he would soon be well enough to rejoin his unit, and he apparently began at this time to doubt if he would survive the war. This is the first indication that DuBose was having second thoughts as to the ultimate success of the Southern cause. He began to plan his marriage as soon as possible. He wrote his future mother-in-law, Mrs. Peronneau, on April 1st, 1863, with a request for her permission and blessing. His letter seems to hint that he felt he was not going to survive the war. Following are a few quotes from that letter, the original of which is still housed at The University of the South:

> I have written to Miss Nannie to try and obtain her and your consent to our marriage without further delay. I quite despair of an early termination of the war, and feel that delaying it until that time or until my ordination- would be equivalent to an indefinite postponement . . . it would be a great satisfaction to me to be married before entering the uncertainties of another long Summer Campaign . . . The Summer Campaign will begin very soon, when nothing short of a wound or a parole will be likely to get me off.

## Vicksburg/Jackson

DuBose and Miss Peronneau married April 30, 1863, during a two-week furlough while the Holcombe Legion was recuperating before moving to Vicksburg, Mississippi. There the legion was to help protect Vicksburg from General Grant's siege. The situation in Mississippi had become so serious that additional troops were ordered from South Carolina, and on May 15th, 1863, the Confederate Secretary of War directed General Beauregard to send Evans' Brigade with all dispatch to aid General Johnston. The governor of South Carolina and the mayor of Charleston complained to President Jefferson Davis that the move stripped the coast of South Carolina of any defense against the Yankees, but Davis was convinced that very few Northern troops were in the state.4 So the Holcombe Legion, under orders, abandoned Charleston and moved toward Vicksburg.

After his small, simple wedding, DuBose again resumed his post as Adjutant of the Holcombe Legion. He rejoined his command in Mississippi near Jackson on the banks of the Pearl River. The Legion then left for Vicksburg under the command of General Joseph Johnston. It found the going rough in the Deep South because of the summer heat and deep dust. Their biggest problems were caused by the Union troops who had gone before them and, according to DuBose, were responsible for "defiling all the sources of water with dead animals, etc." [7] They arrived at the Big Black on the evening of July 3rd and went to sleep fully expecting to attack the rear of Grant's besieging army. They were amazed the next morning when they proceeded to quickly march back the way they had just come, necessitated by the surrender of Vicksburg. The trip was a hurried one: Grant now pursued them back towards Jackson.

**Defense of Vicksburg**

In his orders on May 11, General Grant says that his forces are as far advanced toward Jackson, Mississippi, in an east-west line, as they can be without bringing on a general engagement. On May 15th, he says that Jackson was now in his hands, with Joe Johnston in command. The Confederates retreated in an attempt to join the Vicksburg forces.13 DuBose's Legion occupied the defense lines in front of the city. From there they heard the sounds of sharpshooting and cannon for the next several days, but no fire was aimed directly at them. [7]

During the time of the sieges in Mississippi, the bulk of the time of the ordinary foot soldier was spent in throwing up breastworks against the expected attack from Grant. As an officer, DuBose certainly didn't participate in such mundane activities as breastworks construction but rather limited himself to observation of the work. DuBose told his students years later that at such times his mind was likely to turn to St. Paul. To him, DuBose said, the Epistle to the Romans was the "piece de resistance." He said that "I can distinctly remember lying on my back while men were constructing breastworks, and with closed eyes, constructing for myself the vital spiritual sequence, unity, and completeness of the first eight chapters." [7]

The Southerners who were present at these battles probably had no idea that the fall of Vicksburg, coincidental with the Union victory at Gettysburg, marked perhaps the turning point in the war, and ultimately, the defeat of the Confederacy. Even if he realized this, DuBose and the rest of the legion, and indeed, the rest of the Army of Virginia, was not to accept it fully for some time to come.

As the Holcombe Legion "lay on its arms" with a few days respite, DuBose was able to walk into local Judge Sharkey's abandoned house and library and spend an afternoon reading an autobiography of the Italian painter Leslie. When he left, he kept the book, assuming that the library and house would soon suffer the same fate as other houses and libraries, that is, to be burned to the ground by the invaders. When he found out years later that the house had survived, his conscience troubled him to the point he attempted to return the book but was told to keep it for The University of the South. [7]

Johnston's Army camped at Morton, Mississippi, on July 20th, 1863. The enemy did not follow, except in small force. After burning Brandon, destroying the railroad bridges, and totally burning Jackson on the 23rd of July, Grant returned to Vicksburg. In this campaign, according to Evans, "The marches and countermarches to which they (the Confederate defenders) were subjected in the heat of summer, the men for the most of the time badly supplied with shoes and actually, at times, suffering for water fit to drink, fully tested the spirit and discipline of the brigade." [4]

### Savannah/Charleston

The Holcombe Legion left the confrontation with Grant in Mississippi and returned to the area of Savannah, Georgia, where they were stationed on a small island on the coast. The unit was told that they might be there for some time, so DuBose made plans for his new wife to visit in the quiet camp. But to their surprise, a few days later the Legion was marched into Savannah, boarded a train, and left immediately for Charleston, South Carolina. As William DuBose was leaving Savannah by train, Mrs. DuBose was steaming into that city. On arrival in Charleston the Holcombe Legion was stationed at Mt. Pleasant, before it was moved to a camp on Sullivan's Island. Toward the end of 1863, DuBose received a communiqué that was to change the course of the war, and, ultimately, his life. He received a commission from the Confederate government in Richmond as chaplain in General Kershaw's Brigade. He was ordered to report to Kershaw (then in Greeneville, Tennessee) to fulfill that order.

# Chapter V

"For I suppose, two or three months, I officiated in
that church (Greenville, Tennessee) to the most distinguished
congregation I have ever served, composed mainly of
Officers of the Army from Generals down."

– W.P. DuBose

## WILLIAM PORCHER DUBOSE AS CHAPLAIN
### (1863-1865)

# CHAPTER V

## William P. DUBOSE AS A CHAPLAIN

### Synopsis

William DuBose was about to undergo a drastic transformation. For two years he had been in the trenches, fighting alongside men with whom he had gone to school and with whom he had enlisted in the Holcombe Legion. Now he was to give up that direct involvement in battle with the men in favor of tending to their souls.

DuBose arrived in Mississippi after Vicksburg had surrendered; the command was sent east again, to Savannah. He hoped his wife could join him. But he was quickly moved to Charleston, where he stayed until the late fall of 1863.

At that time, to his surprise and disappointment, DuBose was named a chaplain and was transferred to General Kershaw's brigade. Why was he disappointed? We have to consider that DuBose had been thoroughly trained as a soldier at The Citadel and service as an officer in defense of his country was the absolute best thing a Southerner of the time could do. He had also spent two long grueling years as the adjutant of the Holcombe Legion and had gone through literal hell with his comrades. Now, he was being told to leave the company of these men and leave all the action to which he had been accustomed. He had been a fragile youth, not always blessed with good health, yet there are no mentions in his or others' writings about health problems as a soldier. Perhaps he was enjoying being "one of the guys" even though an officer. Although not yet an ordained minister, he was close. To his friends this was a sufficient peg on which to hang safety for a friend who had done his share of hard service. In December, 1863, he was ordained as a deacon in the Episcopal Church at Camden, South Carolina, and began his ministry to the Army in Greeneville, Tennessee, where the brigade was in winter quarters.

In the Spring of 1864, Kershaw's brigade was ordered to Virginia and played a part in the Wilderness, then Spottsylvania, then at Cold Harbor. When the defense lines were established at Petersburg, the brigade was sent to the Valley of Virginia to assist General Early in his unsuccessful campaign against General Sheridan.

DuBose probably had considerable trepidation about the job change. The Civil War literature has references to other men who underwent this change. These men handled the situation with "on the job training," mostly self-training. New chaplains had observed other chaplains assigned to units with which they had fought in the past. But observing and doing are indeed different. DuBose had been in the seminary about one and one-half years prior to the war, but now he was on his own, freshly ordained as a Deacon in the Episcopal Church. He was to provide moral and spiritual support for men — men who by this time were discouraged and wondering why they were in the situation in which they found themselves.

A Civil War chaplain was expected to do substantially more than simply provide spiritual support. They were also part-time surgeon helpers, teachers, and scavengers and they fulfilled many other tasks. In addition, they had to deal with "hostile" commanding officers, low pay, and substantial in-fighting between denominations. But perhaps this list of potential problems is the same for clergy in civilian life as in the military. DuBose's two years as a chaplain were in a brigade that had seen considerable action in the first two years of the war and was to be heavily involved in many hot-spots until the bitter end.

DuBose provides less information on his activities during his chaplaincy than on his military career. This is true in both his *Reminiscences* [7] and other published autobiographical sketches, such as *Turning Points in My Life.* [6] One wonders why, but I suppose the reason is that being a chaplain, for the most part, is not as exciting to listeners as being a soldier in the front ranks of the battle. One can imagine a grandchild or neighboring child asking, "Tell us about when you were a <u>soldier</u> in the big war . . . " but not, "Tell us about when you were a <u>chaplain</u> in the big war . . ." This dearth of information does limit our ability to understand DuBose's feelings during his conversion from soldier to chaplain. But the few comments he makes in *Reminiscences* are detailed and particularly poignant and certainly reflect his innermost thoughts at that time. To better understand his transformation, I have used a number of secondary sources describing the role of chaplain to the Confederate Army and have fitted these sources to DuBose's comments. I hope this approach will provide a satisfactory understanding of what was happening to William DuBose during these two years of frustration and ultimate defeat of the Confederacy.

## The Transition

DuBose's commission as chaplain with Kershaw's Brigade was procured for him by influential friends in "church and state." To his friends this change was an attempt to provide some measure of safety for DuBose. Because the "influential friends" were Bishop Theodore Davis and General Joseph Kershaw, DuBose had to hurry to comply with the orders.

On July 22nd, 1863, Brigadier General W.G. Evans wrote Assistant Adjutant General S. Cooper in Richmond, Virginia, to request that William P. DuBose receive a promotion to rank of Captain and be named Inspector General in the Adjutant General's Department assigned to General Evans. This information was not mentioned in the many articles, reports, and books about DuBose. Up to that point, William DuBose was listed as a lieutenant on all other army records, including roll call and pay voucher documents.

On August 3, 1863 one Ed. A. Palfrey wrote to General Evans denying a request made by the general. Palfrey stated that "Gen'l Evans Brigade has an Asst. Adjt. Gen'l and but one is allowable." I would guess that General Evans and General Kershaw had tried this avenue first in their attempt to move DuBose off the front line and give him a chance to survive the war.

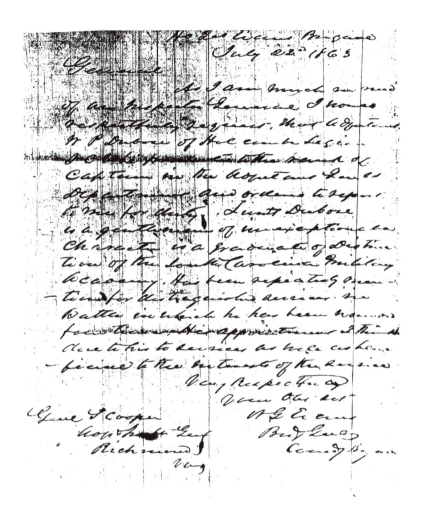

Letter from Military Records of W.P. DuBose, South Carolina Archives

Plate 2

The day after the denial document was received by General Evans on August 4th, General Kershaw wrote a letter to General S. Cooper in Richmond, requesting that DuBose be appointed Chaplain-at-Large for his brigade. The letter says that DuBose is recommended by Bishop Davis of South Carolina and that though three Chaplains are already attached to Kershaw's Brigade, none are from the Episcopal Church. Kershaw states that DuBose is a "gentle man" of the "purest piety of character and conduct of highest attainment and commanding talents." A copy of this letter is shown.

Headquarters wrote back on August 11 and asked Kershaw to determine if DuBose would accept the position as Chaplain. Although I could not find evidence of his response, he obviously indicated he would. On August 29th, Palfrey forwarded Kershaw's request to the Office of the Confederate Secretary of War with a terse statement that "The Law allows Chaplains to Brigades." On September 1st, J.A. Campbell signed the transfer. Getting DuBose back from the field took some time: not until November 1, 1863, did he resign from the position of Adjutant of the Holcombe Legion. Pay vouchers show he was receiving the sum of $100 per month as a Lieutenant for the Confederate Army. He was now about to earn the princely salary of $85 per month as a Chaplain.

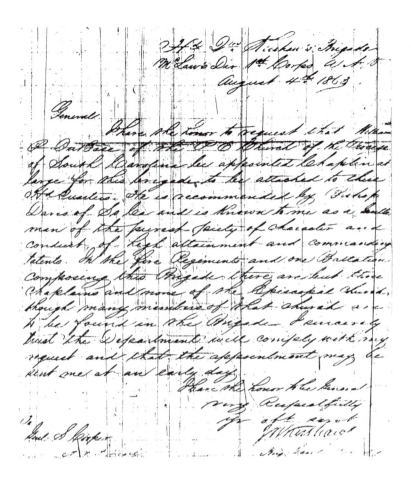

Letter from Military Records of W.P. DuBose, South Carolina Archives

Plate 3

On December 13, 1863, at Grace Church, Camden Bishop
Davis quickly ordained DuBose in a "special service" as a Deacon in
the Episcopal Church. DuBose's original ordination certificates for
the diaconate and the priesthood are in The University of the South
Library, in Sewanee, Tennessee. The Certificate of Ordination as
Deacon, 1863, states he is a Deacon in the Protestant Episcopal
Church, Confederate States of America. When DuBose was
ordained as a priest in 1866, the printed certificate has the words
Protestant Episcopal Church, Confederate States of America, but
someone drew a line through "Confederate," and wrote in "United."
Apparently, although the Southern branch of the Episcopal Church
had been reaccepted into the whole church, no one had sent new
ordination certificates to the Church in South Carolina by that time,
so they simply modified the old Confederate certificates. Following
his ordination as a Deacon, DuBose joined Kershaw's brigade in
Greeneville, Tennessee, and began his ministry there.

Kershaw was wintering in East Tennessee, so DuBose, accompanied by his cousin, Colonel Gaillard, set out on horseback early in
1864 from Winnsboro to ride through South and North Carolina
and Tennessee. While in Mississippi, DuBose bought himself a new
horse, perhaps to replace the horse he had "procured" from the lost
Yankee cavalryman in northern Virginia. He named his new horse
John, and John survived the war along with DuBose. For this ride to
east Tennessee, however, DuBose left John home in South Carolina
to recuperate and borrowed a mare named Mayflower the Second
from his brother Robert. During the trip they nearly encountered
bushwhackers but arrived in Greeneville without incident. DuBose
reported to the vacant headquarters of Kershaw, a large building that
served as an office before the war. DuBose spent the night in his new,
quiet quarters. To his dismay when he awoke the next morning, he
found that "Morgan's men came by in the night and the next morning my horse was missing. I had ridden her through three states, only
to have her stolen on the night of my arrival." [7]

The brigade was off on a temporary expedition, so DuBose settled in and "became domesticated." Kershaw's expedition was
described as being a difficult one, because of the weather:

> The weather had gotten down to two degrees below zero,
> the ground frozen as hard as brick-bats, and the winds
> whistled gaily through our tattered tents, our teeth beating
> tattoo and our limbs shivering from the effects of our
> scanty clothing and shoes. But our wagons were gathering
> in supplies from the rich valleys of the French Broad and
> the Nollachuckey (sic), and while we suffered from cold,
> we generally had provisions sufficient for our want. [14]

During the winter quarters in progress, DuBose was requested to
take charge of the church in Greeneville. He accepted and began his
ministry there. According to his *Reminiscences*, "For I suppose, two
or three months, I officiated in that church to the most distinguished
congregation I have ever served, composed mainly of officers of the
army from generals down." [7] However, the life of domestication in
Greeneville did not last very long. Soon DuBose was beginning his
new role with the Confederate Army as he served as Chaplain-at-
large with Kershaw's Brigade for the next two bloody, bitter years.

## Religion In The Confederate Army

Some background information about religion in the South in general, and in the Confederate army in particular helps us better understand the environment in which DuBose began his ministry.

### Religion in the Confederate Army

Southerners of the nineteenth century were a religious people, and church membership was a mark of respectability. The presence of a clergyman was sought for private functions, and being sent to war with a benediction consisting of a talk and a prayer with his local minister was natural for a Southern soldier. In men's knapsacks, a Bible was the first thing tucked away.

For the first years of the war, religion did not fare well. Services were seldom organized and were poorly attended. Bibles were thrown away with other heavy, unused items from men's knapsacks, and a religious man was taunted by his fellow soldiers as being weak and scared. For two years, the only men interested in religion were the sick or wounded, and many volunteer ministers became discouraged and went home.

The Chaplaincy was poorly organized, and at first there were few Chaplains. One reason was that the organized civilian churches had an early reluctance to send clergymen away from their home parishes to go to the army. For example, the Protestant Episcopal Church of Alabama did not think that the religious needs of the army were primary and thus did not encourage ordained clergy to leave their congregations to become chaplains early in the war. [12] Another reason for this early disinterest in religion was the festive attitude with which the Southern soldier left home to whip the Yankees in short order; no one thought that the war would be long and bloody.

After the close of 1862, that the end result for the Confederacy could ultimately be nothing but defeat was becoming obvious. As the North slowly but surely cut transportation of needed Southern supplies, the only boundless supply of anything that the South could count on was spiritual resources. In the last two years of the war, nothing held the Confederates together more than their faith in God and their belief in the rightness of their cause. No one contributed as much to this situation as the chaplains in the Confederate service.

In the first years of the war, there were chaplains who lacked education or knowledge or zeal. The hardships encountered in following and ministering to the army soon eliminated those who were not conscientious and dedicated. Early, incompetent ministers were characterized by an English visitor as "long-jawed, loud-mouthed ranters . . . offensively loquacious upon every topic of life, save men's salvation." Some soldiers denounced their chaplains on the basis of cowardice. An Alabamian wrote, "We got into a little row with the Yanks a few days ago, and our parson . . . took to his heels when the shells commenced flying and I have not seen him since." [17]

A Southern newspaper in 1862 summarized opinions of those who had little respect for the military chaplains, in the early years of the war, by publishing the following military "catechism":

**Q.** What is the first duty of a chaplain?
**A.** Never to mention the subject of religion to the soldiers.

**Q.** What is the second duty?
**A.** To preach to the regiment only once a year, and not that unless specially requested by the Colonel.

**Q.** What is the third duty?
**A.** To grumble all the time about the smallness of his pay.

During the early years of the war, many chaplains fell prey to the lowered moral standards common in a war setting. They were surrounded by

men who felt that swearing, gambling, drinking, and such forms of entertainment were all that were available to them. All these were considered
sins in those times in the South. The human goal was to be a popular
chaplain, and many of the early chaplains learned to "wink" at the sins
around them. Ironically, they did not become popular but instead lost the
respect of the men and had to leave. The percentage of drop-outs was
high. For example, more than eighty ministers resigned from Confederate
units during one six-month period. [34]

Romero repeats an amusing story told by Bailer regarding the teas-
ing by the Twelfth Virginia Cavalry of their chaplain, recognized by the
men as a pious man, but subject, nonetheless to coarse and typical "military humor": "On one of their marches the adjutant and another officer
(who told the story) suggested that they ride ahead with the chaplain and
surgeon to a house up the road to get some food. This sounded tempt-
ing to the chaplain and surgeon, so off they went and were highly pleased
at the cordial reception given them by two handsomely dressed ladies.
Now it happened that this house was known by all the men of the brigade
(except the chaplain and the surgeon) to be a house of ill-repute. When
the brigade drew near and recognized the horses of their man of God and
man of medicine they raised a shout that was heard for miles around. At
this the ladies suddenly threw their arms around "these innocents" and
gave other demonstrations of a violent affection. The adjutant and other
officer quietly left the house followed by two irate and indignant victims of
the disciple of Jezebel." [12]

Another problem was a lack of understanding between chaplains and
line officers as to what a chaplain's duties were to be. The dispute
became bitter and, in many cases, the line officers would not fill a vacant
office of chaplain, rather than put up with what they considered to be an
inconvenience. The office of chaplain was not popular within the army
because the officers felt that the religious man did not make a good soldier. Not for several years did the army realize that the religious Southern
man made the best soldier.

Barring an occasional skirmish, Sunday was officially holy in the Confederate Army (with the notable exception of The Battle of Shiloh, April, 1862, which began on a Sunday). It was the chaplain's day to lead service. A few officers were unsympathetic towards the chaplains and their services and filled the day with busy work so no time remained for religious service. William DuBose's cousin, Franklin Gaillard, wrote home that, "I went over to see Willie [William DuBose] last Sunday, and they were drilling just the same as any other day." [28]

**_Materials for worship; Official view of Chaplains; The Winning of Souls_**

Church leaders in the South eventually realized the necessity of the spiritual needs of the army, and they instituted movements that exerted much influence. One movement was the passing out of spiritual literature. Few Bibles were printed in the South before the war, and the North soon decided that Bibles were contraband material and refused to continue to ship them to the South. Having depended in the past on the North for Bibles, the South faced the problem of having the supply cut off. Southern ingenuity together with Northern friends cooperated to eventually smuggle in printing plates, and preparations were made to print the first Confederate Bibles. In 1861, the initial copies of these Bibles were printed by Southwestern Publishing House in Nashville, Tennessee. The Tennessee Baptist reported, that, " . . . for the first time the South is independent of the North for the Word of God. Lincoln no longer binds the Word of God." One exception to the Northern blockade was the American Bible Society, which early in the war, sent over 100,000 Bibles to groups responsible for service to the Southern troops. Early in the war, chaplains were active after a battle, going over the battlefield to gather up Bibles left by friend and foe alike for redistribution to the living

Second to Bibles, the most common and widely distributed religious materials were tracts, or leaflets. These publications were pocket-sized and only a few pages long. They addressed subjects as conversion, how to seek religion, how to avoid sin, practical advice on how to maintain the health of body or soul, and how to avoid procrastination.

Today as in 1860, an important part of an Episcopalian's worship is the Book of Common Prayer. As the flow of Bibles to the South from the North ceased, so did the flow of copies of the Prayer Book. Chaplain Kensey J. Stewart, an Episcopalian chaplain, was attached to the 6th North Carolina Regiment. Early in 1863, Stewart arranged for an English printer to publish a Southern Episcopal Book of Common Prayer. This was done, but the ship carrying the books from England was captured by the Federal blockade and the books thrown into the ocean. Stewart returned on a different vessel and reached Richmond with a few copies of the Confederate Episcopal Prayer Book. He delivered these to Mr. John W. Randolph, who had commissioned the publication. Randolph gave copies to Mrs. Robert E. Lee and President Jefferson Davis. [34] The only real difference between the Southern and Northern Prayer Books was that in the Southern edition the word "United" in 'United States of America' was replaced with "Confederate."

Perhaps the major reason for the ultimate success of the chaplain system was the influence of Generals Robert E. Lee and Thomas J. (Stonewall) Jackson. Both men set examples to their men as to the importance of religion in their lives. Lee issued orders concerning the important place religion was to play in the future of the Confederate Army. Also, on May 3, 1861, the Confederate Congress approved Bill Number 102, which included these words: "There shall be appointed by the President such number of chaplains, to serve with the armies of the Confederate States during the existing war, as he may deem expedient; and the President shall assign them to such regiments, brigades or posts as he may deem necessary; and the appointments made as aforesaid shall expire whenever the existing war shall terminate."

A long-running debate broke out in the halls of the Confederate Congress as to the pay of newly appointed chaplains. The amount started at $85 per month, including all allowances. The political battle raged on, and the recommended pay varied between $100 per month and $300 per year. By the time DuBose became a chaplain, the salary had settled at $80 per month plus the rations of a private. Most denominations supplemented this pay, particularly for those chaplains with families at home.

Pay for chaplains eventually included forage for their horses, but this provision was delayed until 1864 and had considerable trouble in passing the Confederate Congress. One legislator wanted it made perfectly clear that this allotment was for forage only and was not intended to provide the chaplain a horse. He had perhaps heard a story about a chaplain who had appropriated a farmer's horse and said his precedent was Jesus Christ who "took an ass from his owner, whereon to ride into Jerusalem." The chaplain was promptly squelched by an officer who said, "You are not Jesus Christ; this is not an ass; you are not on your way to Jerusalem; the sooner you restore that horse to its owner, the better it will be for you." [34]

No regulations were established for chaplains regarding age, education, ecclesiastical endorsement, uniform, carrying of arms, or even the holding of religious services. They had no military rank, and some chaplains were reprimanded early in the war for wearing gaudy or quasi-military garb. The chaplaincy was a regimental institution, and chaplains in higher units of the army had no authority over those in lower units. Chaplains were not transferred from unit to unit without consent, and their carrying of arms although permitted, was generally frowned upon. A number of stories do exist, however, about gun-toting, fighting chaplains who were known to join in battles along with soldiers.

The Confederate chaplains eventually numbered 600, at least two-thirds of whom were under 30 years of age. Of the Protestants, only approximately 193,000 were Episcopalians, but they furnished the highest percentage of chaplains to the war effort.

Eventually, religion flourished in the army. So effective was the work of chaplains on both sides that numerous books have been published about the history of religion during the war. Officers who were perhaps "ungodly by nature" found themselves sandwiched between extremely pious superior officers and humble, religious privates, and thousands of soldiers embraced the Gospel. The campfires were often used to illuminate the pages of the Bible, and religious songs helped fill the spare time of encamped soldiers.

Religious services in the Confederate Army consisted of preaching and prayer meetings. These were usually held on Sunday morning, but frequent changes in schedule were common; an army on the march held its services at night. At times the minister took his place before the campfire with his "congregation" gathered around on logs, stumps, or the ground. As winter came on, soldiers built log tabernacles and furnished them with pulpits, seats, and lights. This was not possible at all encampments, but the zeal of the worshipers allowed them to worship, no matter what the situation or weather. One chaplain told of preaching to Mississippians for forty minutes in a steady rain, and no listener stirred. In one case, a chaplain preached to Virginians in several inches of snow; the men who sat listening were barefoot.

Communion services meant a great deal to the men who were constantly contemplating and facing death. Communion was looked upon as a means of grace, especially preceding a battle. Episcopalians attempted to provide the rite of communion to men on the lines every day.

Singing was popular among the Southerners before the war, and that did not change. Hymns popular with the Confederate soldiers were "All Hail the Power," "Amazing Grace," "How Firm a Foundation," "Jesus Lover of my Soul," "Nearer My God to Thee," "Rock of Ages," "There is a Fountain," and "When I can Read My Title Clear."[35]

Among professions of faith received by ministers were those of Generals Bragg, Anderson, Rodes, Pender, and Paxton. In the spring of 1864, Episcopal Bishop-General Leonidas Polk baptized Generals Hood, Hardee, and Joseph E. Johnston.[17] President Jefferson Davis also became a communicant during the war. Many military units were composed of nothing but ministers or ministerial students. The Ninth Arkansas was known as the "Parsons Regiment" because it included 42 ordained ministers in its ranks.[35]

The Camden, South Carolina, Episcopal Seminary, in which William DuBose had been a student before the war, had to close down with the advent of the war because all the seminarians joined the Confederate Army, and no students remained.

### The Foot-Soldiers View: Preaching, Conversion, and Revivals

For the soldier's body there was medical care, which although inadequate today, was as good as could be expected under the circumstances. For the soldier's soul, there was the haphazard chaplain system. In spite of the early inefficiencies of that system, the soldiers generally took time from their other entertainment activities such as gambling, playing, foraging, and cockfighting to undergo a religious revival. As described in many diaries written by soldiers, this was the way religious revival happened.

At times intense religious interest and revival invaded an entire army. Many soldiers became witnesses to the changes made in them by the preaching of the faithful chaplains who shared with the men (their parishioners) the dangers, hardships, and even the occasional pleasures of long campaigns.

All the books written about the Civil War that began as soldier's diaries contain references about the impact of religion and the ministers and chaplains that served alongside the men. The following pages present a few of the many quotations by the men who served both armies, North and South.

Corporal James Henry Gooding, Company C, 54th Massachusetts Colored, March 30th, 1863: "And here I may remark that every officer in camp appears to take an interest in the speedy and correct discipline of the men; neither are they lacking in regard for the religious welfare of the men, receiving the proffers of religious men willingly, who desire to make any remarks beneficial to the men. Rev. Wm. Jackson is here, and is to act as chaplain pro tem.  Mr. Rickers, City Missionary, from Boston, preached yesterday afternoon, and Rev. Mr. Jackson in the afternoon."[36]

Religious revivals were the norm for the soldiers. As inactivity became the standard for a long "wintering," some relief was found in reading and the other recreations of camp life.  Revivalism became intense after the victory at Chancellorsville and did not slow down until Gettysburg. In the area of Dalton, Georgia, revivals were quite common. Gettysburg and Vicksburg may have dampened the military and patriotic spirits of the Confederates somewhat, but the losses did not destroy the spirit of the revival movement.  Revivals lost their steam during active campaigns but regained momentum when units stopped for rest and reorganization.

The final years of the war were marked by many meetings, conversions, baptisms, and log chapels.  Various organizations such as Army churches, Christian societies, Bible study groups, and Sunday schools continued to push spiritual growth among the Confederate soldiers. Prayer meetings and preaching claimed the interest of those religiously inclined. Kershaw's Division, where DuBose was assigned, began to have daily preaching in July, 1864, when interest became obvious throughout the brigade.

The winter of 1863-1864 in Dalton, Georgia, was peaceful for the soldiers of the "Orphan Brigade," the First Kentucky Brigade, CSA, which got its name from the fact that its members were orphaned from their home state. Diary writer John S. Jackman of that Brigade took part in the religious revival that swept through the army: "January 17th- Sunday. Went to church in the forenoon and heard a good sermon.  There are three Protestant churches in Dalton- Baptist, Methodist and Presbyterian. There is also a very neat Catholic church in town.  Of Sundays, these churches are generally full to overflowing, with soldiers.  Chaplains from the army generally officiate.  Many soldiers go to church just to get sight of a lady."[37]

Warren Wilkinson, in *Mother May You Never See the Sights I Have Seen*, which provides the history of the 57th Massachusetts Veteran Volunteers in the Army of the Potomac, made a number of comments regarding the importance of religion to the foot soldier. For example: "Fear was weakness, and weakness was not tolerated by Civil War Soldiers. Nevertheless, they were human, and talk around the campfires could not help but be strained as each of the boys lost himself in his thoughts and dwelled inwardly on his own well-being and loved ones at home. This would be life's last day for many of them, and they all knew it. Hasty, sentimental letters were written, and prayers silently said. The Irish and others of the Roman Catholic faith in the regiment sought out chaplain priests in the division for confession and absolution, and Reverend Dashiell ministered to the Protestants." [38]

All was not serene between the differing religions of the soldiers; what was comfort for some was not understood or appreciated by others. Ministers were afraid that a relationship between themselves and ministers of other denominations would bring down the wrath of civilian church authorities. This was true early, when it was felt that the struggle would last only a few months. For many years prior to the war, denominations were accustomed to threatening one another with secession or expulsion upon the slightest pretext, so it was not hard to understand preachers' non-fraternization while in the army. It was difficult for preachers steeped in sectarianism to avoid offending soldiers sensitive to differences in doctrines.

Wilkinson goes on to say: "Roman Catholic chaplains moved through the Federal formations absolving the Irish and other soldiers of that faith. The self-righteous Methodists, Episcopalians, and Baptists thought the scene contemptible and vile, and they sneered at the Popery." [38] General Stonewall Jackson had a major impact on these interdenominational squabbles, when he issued a statement saying: "Denominational distinctions should be kept out of view, and not touched upon. And, as a general rule, I do not think that a chaplain who would preach denominational sermons should be in the army . . . I would like to see no question asked in the army of what denomination a chaplain belongs to; but let the question be, Does he preach the Gospel?"[35]

Denominational differences were minimized when possible, particularly after Jackson's statement. On one occasion, a visiting minister reported, "We had a Presbyterian sermon, introduced by Baptist services, under the direction of a Methodist chaplain, in an Episcopalian church."[17]

Packages received from home were many times the highlight of the day for the lonely soldiers. Food, which provided an alternative to dreary army food, was always appreciated. Wilkinson describes an attitude toward a different type of package: "Far less appreciated (than food, medicine, tobacco) were the donations from the Christian Commission, which sent almost exclusively religious literature that many of the hard-core veterans considered worthless except for lighting campfires. Bibles, too, were distributed in large quantities throughout the army by this organization, but even though almost all of the soldiers held a deep respect for the Holy Book, they were much more in need of refreshments of the flesh."[38]

The Civil War diary and letters of Elisha Hunt Rhodes, Colonel of the 2nd Rhode Island Volunteers, were collected in a volume entitled *All For the Union*. Rhodes mentions the importance of religion to his unit frequently throughout his writings: "September 6th, 1863- We are having considerable religious interest in our Regiment, and I pray God that it may continue. Soldiers are not the worst men in the world, but they are very careless in regard to matters of religion. We have had no chaplain for many months and consequently no regular services. Our last Chaplain never did any good in the Regiment. About three weeks ago three of our men who are Christians attended a religious meeting at one of the camps in Gen. Wheaton's Brigade. On the way home they knelt down in the woods and prayed that God bless our Regiment. The next week six of them met for prayer, and last week about thirty were present. Tonight I was invited to join them. I accepted and made an address. About fifty men were present at first, but they soon began to come into the grove, and soon nearly every officer and man of our Regiment was listening to the service. I never saw such a prayer service before, and I know the Spirit of the Lord was with us." [39]

Sermons delivered to the foot soldier, whether Northern or Southern, were normally presented in simple terms. These sermons were criticized as appealing to the "lower class of the regiment," but as the chaplains viewed Jesus as their precedent, and as He preached mainly to the lower classes, this criticism did not bother the chaplains. The average sermon was short for the times, some fifteen to thirty minutes. Subjects receiving the most frequent attention were the necessity of repentance on the part of the sinner, the uncertainties of life, the ultimate consequence of sin, the terrors of hell, the importance of retaining a Christian vigilance, the omnipotence of God, and the totality of divine mercy.

The Confederate chaplain's prevailing style was evangelistic, and most worship services centered around preaching. The uneducated clergy gave the most emphasis to preaching, but Episcopalians, Lutherans, and Roman Catholics also preached. [34] At times the preachers from the outside forgot themselves and the audience to whom they preached. Sam Watkins in *Co. Aytch*, relates such an incident, with his particular style of humor and justice for such people who, perhaps need "comeuppance:" "One Sabbath morning it was announced that an eloquent and able LL.D. from Nashville, was going to preach, and as the occasion was an extremely solemn one, we were anxious to hear this divine preach from God's Holy Word; and as he was one of the "big ones," the whole army was formed in close column and stacked their arms . . . Everything looked solemn. The trees looked solemn, the scene looked solemn, the men looked solemn, even the horses looked solemn. You may be sure, reader, that we felt solemn. The Reverend LL.D. had prepared a regular war sermon before he left home, and of course had to preach it, appropriate or not appropriate . . . I lost the further run of his prayer, but regret very much that I did so, because it was so grand and fine that I would liked very much to have kept such an appropriate prayer for posterity . . . In fact, he was so "high larnt" that I don't think any one understood him but the Generals. The Colonels might every now and then have understood a word, and maybe a few of the Captains and Lieutenants, because Lieutenant Lansdown told me he understood every word the preacher said, and further informed me that it was none of your one-horse, old-fashioned country prayers that privates knew anything about, but was bang-up, first-rate, orthodox . . . I remember that after he got warmed up a little, he began to pitch in on the Yankee nation, and gave them particular fits as to their genealogy . . . He said that he and his brethren would fight the Yankees in this world, and if God permit, chase their frightened ghosts in the next, through fire and brimstone. About this time we heard the awfullest racket, produced by some wild animal tearing through the woods towards us, and the cry, "Look out! look out! hooie! hooie! hooie! look out!" and there came running right through our midst a wild bull, mad with terror and fright, running right over and knocking down the divine, and scattering Bibles and hymn books in every direction. The services were brought to a close without the doxology." [16]

Sam Watkins goes on with another story of a later time and manages to turn an ironic and sad story into a positive and touching occurrence, so far as the common foot soldier was concerned: "At this place (Dalton) a revival of religion sprang up, and there was divine service every day and night. Soldiers became serious on the subject of their soul's salvation. In sweeping the streets and cleaning up, an old tree had been set on fire, and had been smoking and burning for several days, and nobody seemed to notice it. That night there was service as usual, and the singing and sermon were excellent . . . As it was the custom to "call up mourners," a long bench had been placed in position for them to kneel down at. Ten of them were kneeling at this mourner's bench, pouring out their souls in prayer to God, asking Him for forgiveness of their sins, and for the salvation of their souls . . . when the burning tree, without any warning, fell with a crash right across the ten mourners, crushing and killing them instantly. God had heard their prayers. Their souls had been carried to Heaven. Hereafter, henceforth, and forevermore, there was no more marching, battling, or camp duty for them. By order of the General, they were buried with great pomp and splendor, that is, for those times . . . The beautiful burial service of the Episcopal Church was read by Rev. Allen Tribble . . . " [16]

### The Job of an Army Chaplain

The life of a chaplain into which William DuBose was thrust was not an easy one. The chaplain normally served a regiment, although in some cases, attempted to serve an entire brigade. He regularly held services and attempted to make himself available to the soldiers who needed spiritual direction. Many chaplains kept records about the souls with whom they were entrusted. Care of the sick and wounded was a primary responsibility of the chaplain, and this care included writing a letter home to inform loved ones that their soldier had been killed or wounded. Chaplains wrote letters for illiterate soldiers and some held classes to fight illiteracy.

The chaplain shared all of the hardships that his flock suffered. During active campaigns and marching he slept on the same ground and ate the same scanty food. When fighting began the chaplain would take a place near the ambulances or field hospitals to be quickly available to the wounded.

Many chaplains had to take up arms in stressful situations. Several were cited for gallantry under fire and some were killed in action. R. H. McKim was a man like W. P. DuBose who laid aside the musket and took up the prayer book to become a chaplain. He became chaplain of a Virginia cavalry regiment. His presence as a minister rather than as a soldier was a bit of a shock to the soldiers at first. The first time he served as chaplain one soldier called out, "Hello Parson, are you going with us into battle?" "Oh, yes," replied McKim, "I'm an old infantry soldier–I don't mind these little cavalry skirmishes." A veteran cavalryman rose in his stirrup and said, "That's right Paason. You stick to us, and we'll stick to you!" [17]

Fulfilling a chaplain's duty was at times hazardous to chaplain and men alike. A Baptist chaplain in Kershaw's Brigade gave an account of a service made memorable by a novel occurrence. He, a Methodist, and a Methodist Episcopal minister were all engaged in administering the rite of baptism to three groups of young men when minie balls whizzed through the congregation and lodged themselves in a hill to the rear.

The care of the men on the line was the first priority of the chaplain, but he was also responsible for those in confinement. Many unfortunate chaplains had the experience of hearing the iron doors clang shut behind them, not an enjoyable sound no matter how brief the stay. However, such conditions presented an opportunity to preach the power of God to open prison doors. Chaplains paid special attention to prisoners in confinement while awaiting execution. If a prisoner were not already a Christian, special efforts were made to correct that situation prior to his execution. William DuBose had the unfortunate duty of such a task late in the war. He tells the story in his *Reminiscences,*

> This brings me up to the moment of the surrender of Lee. Just before this took place, I had one of the most painful little duties to perform that I think was <u>ever</u> imposed upon me. It is a curious thing–Just to stop for a moment. There was at that time in Orangeburg a genuine Dutch settlement. Well, one of the latest levies of troops was from that region and the particular regiment, i.e., 20th or 25th South Carolina regiment, Kitt's, was a large one of new men, who began to desert. General Johnston saw that this must be stopped. It was hard because they were deserting mainly just to see how things were at home, Sherman having passed their homes. Some half dozen were caught, court-martialed, and sentenced to be shot and I was told to inform and prepare them for execution. It was the most awful thing I was ever asked to do, the worst I ever experienced. Fortunately, the surrender came and the sentence was not executed. [7]

As the war continued the casualty list grew steadily longer, and the number of surgeons decreased. This meant additional work for the Southern chaplains because the hospitals were inadequate for all the wounded that were transported into Richmond and other Southern cities. Many times the wounded were left lying in cold boxcars. DuBose says in *Turning Points* that following the Battle of the Wilderness, his duties were primarily in the hospitals and in private ministrations. [6] The chaplains had to take matters into their own hands by such means as the creation of wayside hospitals, with the assistance of church groups.

At times the wounded on the field of battle had to lie for days where they fell. The chaplains tended them as best their meager supplies would allow by covering the soldiers with blankets and giving them water; some chaplains even carried wine to provide some semblance of relief from the pain of the wounds. The chaplain also had the unpleasant task of holding the soldier as the surgeons performed necessary amputations without anesthesia. If the soldier were dying, the chaplain recorded notes to send to the loved ones at home. This was particularly important during the closing months of the war, when the political offices had practically ceased and the newspapers, which had previously served as the notification medium, suspended publications.

Every letter that came to a deceased soldier was opened, read, and responded to by the chaplain. Throughout the war the closest supporters of the chaplain were the surgeons. When hospitals were short on space, the surgeon asked the chaplain for the location of the nearest alternative, and they in turn directed the chaplain to soldiers in most need of ministration.

Many chaplains taught classes on reading and writing or, if time permitted, arranged for other soldier-teachers. The textbooks most commonly used were McGuffey's *First Reader* and the Bible. I have in my possession a copy of Kersham's *Grammar*, published in 1857 and carried throughout the war by my great-grandfather and namesake, John W. Morris,. Morris served with the Confederate Seventh Kentucky Volunteers–Mounted Infantry. In the front of this small, leather-covered book he proudly wrote, "J.W. Morris–my book–cost–50 cents." Morris gave or loaned the book to his brother, Moses Franklin Morris. Moses Morris died of a "congestive chill" on April 10, 1864, as he returned to the army following a furlough. My grandmother told me that my great-grandfather proudly carried the book during the war and studied his way through the lessons when "things settled down for a bit."

## Kershaw's Brigade From 1863 to 1865

Kershaw's Brigade participated in the Battle of Gettysburg before William DuBose joined them in winter camp in Tennessee. DuBose's travels as a chaplain, from Charleston to Petersburg, are shown in Figure 9. An amusing story is told of the trip by train on September 8, 1863, to Richmond from Gettysburg. Kershaw's men were loaded into and onto boxcars–many men sat and stood on top as well as inside. The boxcars, like those on all troop trains, little more than skeleton cars were soon stripped. All but the framework was cut loose with knives and axes: the weather was warm and the troops wanted to see outside and witness the fine country and scenery that lay along the route. Those inside could not stand the idea of being shut up in a boxcar while their comrades on top were cheering and yelling at the waving of handkerchiefs and flags in the hands of the pretty women and hats being thrown in the air by the old men and boys along the railroad as the trains sped through the Carolinas and Georgia.

On September 12, 1863, Kershaw's Brigade detrained at Catoosa Station, Georgia, and marched to nearby Ringgold. Their advance from there did not begin until the night of September 19, after the close of the first day of the Battle of Chickamauga. General Kershaw commanded two brigades at Chickamauga–Humphrey's and his own. On the left wing on the 20th Kershaw was in the thick of the fight. Kershaw said later of that struggle:

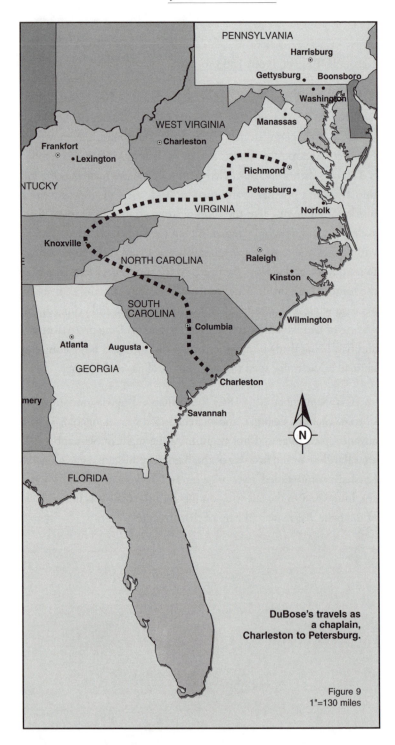

DuBose's travels as
a chaplain,
Charleston to Petersburg.

Figure 9
1"=130 miles

This was one of the heaviest attacks on a single point I ever witnessed! The brigades went in magnificent order. For an hour and a half the struggle continued with unabated fury. It terminated at sunset. It was held with splendid courage and was defended by all the forces of the center and right which could be rallied . . . [14]

In winter of 1863 Kershaw's Brigade was moved to the Knoxville, Tennessee, area, where they were to remain until spring. The men hoped for only minor skirmishes. On November 26, in Knoxville, with Longstreet in a council of war, they decided to remain in front of Knoxville, keeping Burnside away. The troops left in the driving rain on December 3 and 4. This group of soldiers, who DuBose was about to join, was a proud bunch. They had participated in most of the major campaigns and battles in the eastern war theatre. Dickert described his fellow soldiers as follows:

South Carolinians took on in a great measure the inspirations of their French Huguenot ancestors and the indomitable courage of their Scotch and German forefathers of the Revolution. They were impulsive, impetuous, and recklessly brave in battle, and were the men to storm breastworks and rush to the cannon's mouth at the head of a "forlorn hope." They possibly might not stay as long in a stubbornly contested battle as some from other States, but would often accomplish as much in a few minutes by the mad fury of their assault as some others would accomplish in as many hours. They were the Ironsides of the South, and each individual felt that he had a holy mission to fulfill. There were no obstacles they could not surmount, no position they would not assail. Enthusiasm and self-confidence were the forte of South Carolinians, and it was for them to raise the Rebel yell and keep it up while the storm of battle raged fierce and furious. They were the first to raise the banner of revolt, and right royally did they sustain it as long as it floated over the Southland. [14]

As stated in a report dated January 14 from Union Colonel Palmer on January 10, 1864, DuBose was with Kershaw's Brigade under the command of General Longstreet, on the north side of the French Broad River near Dandridge, Tennessee. Kershaw's Division was ordered to leave on the 15th for Morristown, Tennessee, and then on February 25 to move on to Greeneville, where they made camp within two or three miles of the town. [13]

In a letter home to his wife in February, 1864, William DuBose's cousin, Franklin Gaillard, mentions a side trip that he and DuBose took from their camp near New Market, Tennessee:

> Willie (William DuBose) and myself had a very pleasant trip. The first evening we stopped at Mrs. Fanny Means intending to spend only a few minutes, but they would not listen to our leaving so we yielded the point and spent the night . . . We rode on and the next day at dinner stopped at a house to rest and feed. We found the people very kind and hospitable . . . That evening we stopped and spent the night at a house a few miles this side of Unionville. When we were coming away I tried to get him to receive pay but the old gentleman stopped me by saying there were two things he wished to die with his conscience clear of, one was charging a soldier, the other was charging a preacher. [28]

On March 13, 1864, the long wintering was over: Kershaw received an order from Assistant Adjutant-General Sorrel to prepare to move early on the morning of the 14th to meet a probable advance on the part of the enemy in the vicinity of Midway, Tennessee. A second order, received at 5:30 A.M. on the 14th, ordered the move. However, the threatened action apparently did not occur because the

Division was ordered back to the Greeneville area on March 19. Two weeks later, on April 2, Kershaw was recommended for promotion to head General McLaws' Division. General Longstreet referred to Kershaw as "prompt, and gallant, and intelligent, and is the senior brigadier of the division and of the corps proper." [13]

In the spring of 1864 DuBose reports that the brigade broke up their winter camp and began preparations to defend Richmond against Grant. Joseph W. Kershaw had been a Brigadier General since February 1862 and had been distinguished in every battle in which he had participated. Kershaw was supported by Lieutenant Colonel Franklin Gaillard with General Micah Jenkins commanding his own brigade, and others.

## The Wilderness Campaign

The Wilderness Campaign was really one long prolonged battle that lasted from May 4 1864, when Grant crossed the Rapidan, to June 14, when he crossed the James. The pattern of the campaign was clear. To get to Richmond, Grant had to whip Lee's Army. Lee's task was to tangle Grant up in the Wilderness and destroy him. Ultimately, Grant's losses in the battles were 55,000, Lee's about half that many. Who won? Lee prevented Grant from breaking his lines, saved Richmond, and forced Grant to fall back on siege. However, Grant punished Lee's Army to such an extent that they never really recovered. Grant had prepared the way for the subsequent attack on Richmond through Petersburg, from the south.

When Longstreet organized a front line, the whipped Third Corps had to pass through Kershaw's men on their withdrawal to the rear and safety. Kershaw's men showed no pity on their comrades. "Do you belong to Lee's Army?" they yelled. Then, "You don't look like the men we left here," and "You're worse than Bragg's men!" Longstreet pushed to attack. Up and down the line dashed Kershaw. "Now, my old Brigade," he cried, "I expect you to do your duty!" Slowly, Kershaw advanced; the Federals were pushed back to their beginning position. Part of Kershaw's Brigade helped with the flanking movement through the woods, eventually breaking the enemy on the Confederate right. [14]

Later that afternoon, Longstreet was accidentally struck in the throat by a Confederate minie ball and three members of his staff were killed in the same way. Kershaw dashed into the confusion-"They are fri-e-en-nds!" he cried in a voice that everyone heard. Friendly fire from Mahone's Confederate Brigade of the Third Corps had temporarily struck down Robert E. Lee's "Old War Horse."14 According to General Kershaw, Mahone's men on hearing the shout, " . . . instantaneously realized the position of things and fell on their faces where they stood." [13]

On May 4, DuBose's brigade arrived at the Battle of the Wilderness just in time to take part in the fighting. DuBose, now serving as a chaplain, was not in the actual fighting anymore, but was never far from it. His friend and cousin, Franklin Gaillard of the Second South Carolina Regiment, told DuBose that he had a premonition that he would not survive the next battle. Prior to the battle he gave DuBose a package to send home in the event of his death. His premonition came true: he was killed along with his servant. Kershaw, in his description of the battle, says Lieutenant Colonel Franklin Gaillard was riding with General Jenkins when a mistaken volley from his own men, the same that mortally wounded Gaillard, killed Jenkins " . . . with a fearful wound." Kershaw reported the death of Colonel James D. Nance and stated that "both (Nance and Gaillard) were gentlemen of education, position and usefulness in civil life and highly distinguished in the field." DuBose buried Gaillard along with Colonel Means (Third South Carolina Regiment) and General Micah Jenkins. Means and Jenkins had been his friends from The Citadel days.[7] Jenkins was later honored by the following resolution of the Board of his alma mater, which read:

> Whereas, It hath pleased Almighty God, the disposer of all events, in an inscrutable degree of Providence, to remove from scenes of useful, glorious, and successful action, Brigadier-General Micah Jenkins, who fell in the discharge of duty, at the battle of the 'Wilderness', on the 6th day of May last; therefore, be it:  Resolved unanimously, That in the death of General Jenkins, South Carolina mourns the loss of one of her noblest, most patriotic and accomplished citizens, and the army of our country a brave, energetic and skillful officer.

The day after the closing of the battle DuBose stopped alongside a small brick church to minister to a sick man and hung his knapsack, containing Gaillard's message for home, in a tree outside the church. Unfortunately, the knapsack was stolen; DuBose later delivered the message verbally to his relatives.

## The Battle of Spotsylvania

General Grant withdrew from Lee's front but was then confronted by Lee again at Spotsylvania Courthouse. Lee issued orders for Dick Anderson to take Kershaw's and Field's divisions and to start before 3:00 A.M. for the courthouse. The orders were clear–get there before the enemy did. DuBose reported that the command to which he was attached was the first to arrive on the new battlefield. He observed General J.E.B. Stuart retarding the enemy's advance, and the infantry, that consisted of the new arriving troops, formed in a slender line. Anderson ordered Kershaw to file to the left and assist Fitz Lee. To the north was a large pile of split rails. Kershaw's veterans sprang forward without waiting for a command and reached the rails 60 scant yards ahead of the Yankees. The Confederates crouched behind the pile, and opened fire. The Union soldiers still thought that cavalry was present instead of infantry and continued to rush forward. The slight protection of the rails still allowed the charging Union troops to rush over some of the prone Southern troops, and, according to DuBose:

> . . . a number of our men were bayoneted in the back. At a temporary hospital . . . I saw a man by the name of Percival from Columbia, South Carolina, with a bayonet wound in his back and a corresponding one in the breast in front, both made by the same bayonet. The amazing thing to me was, that that man was in the ranks again in what seemed to me not more than a few weeks." [7]

The Federal infantry showed no inclination to break off the fight after only one repulse. Stern resistance by Kershaw's infantry, stubborn artillery fire, and extremely hard fighting by the cavalry kept the enemy at a distance. Kershaw's men were spread thin. As the day wore on, the hot sun took an additional toll, as did the woods set afire by muzzle flashes and the choking dust raised by marching men. As the Federals began a final assault, Ewell arrived and lined up to the right of Kershaw. Together, they successfully held off the attack.

During this time DuBose was apparently acting in the role of spiritual advisor, in addition to his other duties as chaplain. He describes an incident, listening to a captain, whom he met while both were captives in Fort Delaware Federal Prison, " . . . pouring out his heart to me in a matter of personal confidence–an affair with a young lady . . ." [7]

Affairs of the heart, however, do not slow down the affairs of war. According to DuBose, General Grant withdrew from Lee's front and was again confronted by Lee at Cold Harbor.

On May 11, 1864, William Porcher DuBose's name is mentioned in the Annual Proceedings of the 75th Annual Convention of the Protestant Episcopal Church in South Carolina, which was held at the Church of the Advent, Spartanburg, South Carolina. The proceedings state that: "William P. DuBose along with six others are entitled to seats but not votes." DuBose's assignment is listed as "William P. DuBose (Deacon) Chaplain in the Army." On May 12, 1864, "The Committee" recommended to Bishop L.F. Guerry that W.P. DuBose be recommended for "Deacons orders." DuBose had already been hurriedly ordained by Bishop Davis on December 13, 1863, in a "Special Ordination" so that he could serve as a chaplain rather than return to active duty as a soldier. This recommendation, therefore, was intended only to clean up the paperwork.

On May 16, Kershaw's Brigade was reported in reserve at Smith's Mill. Then, at Cold Harbor on June 1st, Kershaw's Brigade was heavily involved in battles and Kershaw's line was furiously attacked. Late in the attack Kershaw brought up the Second and Third South Carolina, regained lost ground, and captured a stand of colors. On June third, the battle began early and strong enemy forces were massed on Kershaw's front. According to Kershaw, "Assault after assault is made and each time repulsed."[4] General Robert E. Lee, in his report of June 3, reported that during the furious fighting, "General Kershaw . . . met with great steadiness and repulsed in every instance." [13]

## The Siege at Petersburg

On June 16, 1864, near Petersburg, Virginia, Army Headquarters were on the south side of the James River. Kershaw's Division was placed north of the James with Powell Hill's Third Corps and most of the cavalry, a total of about 21,000 troops. By the night of June 16, Grant ferried his men across the James River, and settled down to besiege Petersburg. His strategy was effective. He pushed his lines to the west, forcing Lee to extend his lines. Because Grant's forces outnumbered Lee's two to one, eventually the thinly-stretched gray line was spread too far. It took nine months, but the line snapped the next spring.

On June 17, 1864, Kershaw's troops were ordered to march from their camp near Chaffin's Bluff to Petersburg in order to reinforce Beauregard's troops. At 3:00 A.M. on the 18th, as they moved to Petersburg followed by Field, Kershaw relieved Bushrod Johnson's division, and Field took position on Kershaw's right. Beauregard's troops worked all night on new breastworks, consisting of new trenches 800 yards closer to the city than the old trenches. A night's labor completed the exhaustion of Beauregard's men. When they saw morning sun on the bayonets of Kershaw's Division and realized they were about to be relieved, they alternately cheered and wept.

## Petersburg and the Defense of Richmond

Confederate General G.T. Beauregard discussed deployment of troops in the vicinity of Petersburg, Virginia: "General Kershaw's division, which proved to be the vanguard of General Lee's army, reached Petersburg early Saturday morning, June 18th; it numbered about 5000 men, and by my orders, was placed on the new line already occupied by our forces with its right on or near the Jerusalem plank-road, extending across the open field and bending back toward the front of the cemetery. Field's division, of about equal strength, came in some two hours after Kershaw's. It had not yet been assigned to its place on the line when Lee in person arrived at 11:30 o'clock on that day." [19]

On July 23, 1864, Kershaw and his troops moved to the north side of the James, to assist in the outer defenses of the capitol. On July 27, part of Kershaw's Division attacked successfully from the position at Chaffin's Bluff that they had taken several days earlier. However, on July 28, Kershaw's men had to retreat in far greater haste than glory, with the loss of 300 prisoners and several stands of colors. According to Confederate Secretary of War J. A. Seddon, Kershaw lost at least four pieces of artillery in this retreat. The guns were twenty-pounder Parrotts of Graham's battery, three of which had been captured from the Yankees at Winchester and one at Harper's Ferry. This skirmish was known as Deep Bottom, and on July 30, Kershaw re-crossed the James River. [13]

## Northern Virginia

Following Spotsylvania and Deep Bottom, DuBose states that Anderson's division, including DuBose's brigade–Kershaw's Infantry Division–was ordered to the Valley of Virginia to assist General Early in his campaign against General Sheridan in August 1864. As DuBose participated in the quiet ride with Kershaw toward the confrontations, he pulled from his ammunition box a little blue and gold volume of Tennyson's poetry that Nannie had given him at the beginning of the war. He recalls in his *Reminiscences,*

> Many a day, with a leg crossed over the pommel of my saddle, as we wound our slow and romantic way through the mountains of Virginia, I drank in the music and sentiment of the 'Songs', or pondered over the mysteries and questionings of 'In Memoriam' . . . Throughout the war, Tennyson was my Bible of humanity, as my New Testament was of divinity. [7]

Kershaw's Brigade, along with DuBose, entered the valley by way of the pass at Front Royal and succeeded " . . . after some maneuvering and fighting in drawing Sheridan out of the valley." [7] On August 12 Kershaw's Division moved from Mitchell's Station toward Culpepper and on August 18 to Winchester. A dispatch from Union General Sheridan on August 17 indicates that the Battles of Third Winchester and Fisher's Hill were part of the maneuvering and fighting discussed by DuBose. These troops at the outset were to operate east of the Blue Ridge. On September 3, 1864, about 4:30 P.M., according to a report from Union General Phil Sheridan, Kershaw's Division attacked Union General Crook on the Berryville Pike near Berryville and was beaten. Kershaw sustained a loss of 50 captured and over 200 killed or wounded. [13]

Things did not improve: on the 13th of September, according to a dispatch from Sheridan, Kershaw's Division was attacked by

General Wilson and the Eighth South Carolina Regiment with sixteen officers and 145 men were captured, along with their battle flag. On September 19, Kershaw was on an expedition to resist the enemy east of the Blue Ridge in Fauquier and Culpepper counties. They were ordered to Petersburg, but halfway there were hurried back into the valley, where Sheridan was once again in control. According to a dispatch from Colonel Schoonmaker of the Fourteenth Pennsylvania Cavalry, Kershaw's Division was virtually shoeless and a large number of the infantry were without arms. On September 26, Kershaw's Division traveled from Swift Run Gap to Brown's Gap and on to Waynesboro. On October 13 Kershaw was involved in skirmishes at Hupps' Hill near Strasburg. Kershaw, his chaplain W.P. DuBose, and the ragged men, rapidly dwindling in numbers, were rapidly ending the end of effective resistance.

### Cedar Creek

DuBose's travels as a chaplain from Petersburg to the conclusion of the war are shown in Figure 10. The climax of the fighting was on October 18, 1864, after the losses of the previous month, came the painful Battle of Cedar Creek. Kershaw's Division marched through Strasburg, turned northeast, crossed Cedar Creek at Bowman's Mill, and struck north against the left of the force Gordon was to attack in the front. Kershaw was to start at 5:00 A.M., just before daybreak, on the 19th.

At 4:30 that morning, Confederate General Jubal Early ordered Kershaw across the creek to surprise the sleeping Yankee camp. No opposition was encountered. The troops sprang forward and cleared the camp. The threat of a cavalry attack forced Kershaw to organize his line hurriedly. By 4:30 P.M., the enemy launched a swift, oblique attack on the weak left. Most of the Confederates gave way and started for the rear. Panic was starting to show. After the initial win by

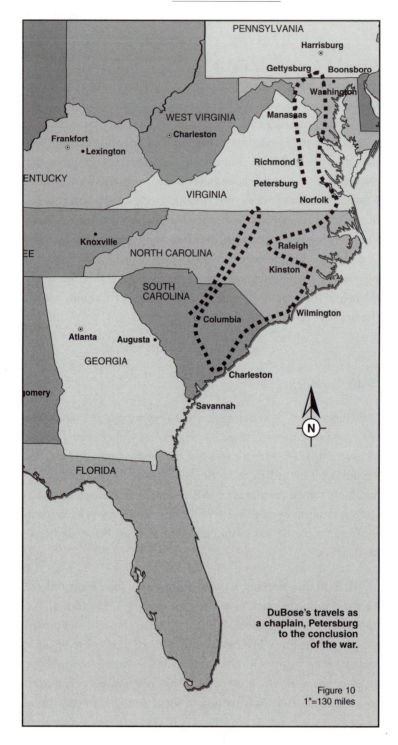

DuBose's travels as
a chaplain, Petersburg
to the conclusion
of the war.

Figure 10
1"=130 miles

Kershaw in which he captured 1,300 prisoners and 18 pieces of artillery, Sheridan's Ride turned the tide and routed the Confederates. Kershaw ultimately lost 205 men. According to a report by Union Colonel Kidd, Kershaw's division, which had faced Kidd's, was utterly broken and scattered. [13]

Following this decisive loss at Cedar Creek, DuBose, like the rest of Kershaw's Division and the remnants of the Army of Virginia, became discouraged with what appeared to be the ultimate conclusion of not only the present battle, but indeed, the war. When the defeated and exhausted Brigade at long last rested at about midnight on October 19, DuBose could not sleep. "The end of the world," he wrote, "was upon me as completely as upon the Romans when the barbarians had overrun them." [6] He later presented a poignant picture in his *Reminiscences*:

> Kershaw's Brigade, which had never slept behind a field of battle, but always on it or before it, slept that night fifteen miles behind one. To others besides myself I think that night's experience was the turning point of the war. The point of experience through which many like myself passed at that time was this. It was a remarkable thing, but I believe it's true, that the ordinary Confederate soldier up to this time never conceived the possibility of ultimate failure. The soldier almost always engaged in action, has no time for reflection or thought, and the Confederate soldier considered himself generally successful and victorious. The resources of the world were behind us, and the time was at hand when we began to feel the result. To me–that night!–I felt as if everything was gone! [7]

DuBose wrote again of this night and of his experience in his published memoir, *Turning Points in My Life*. On that night DuBose made a decision for which Episcopalians are grateful. He wrote:

The actual issue was all upon me that fateful night in which, under the stars, alone on the planet, without home or country or any earthly interest or object before me, my very world at an end, I re-devoted myself wholly and only to God, and to the work and life of His Kingdom, whatever and wherever that might be. [6]

Kershaw's Brigade rejoined its old corps commander Jubal Early, on November 15, to the north of James River. According to a Union report, they passed Richmond on or about November 18 and were camped two and one-half miles below Richmond between the stage road and the Charles City Road. A report to General Robert E. Lee on November 22 stated that, "Kershaw's troops are not yet in prime condition." [13] This was certainly a reflection of the devastating losses they had recently suffered. On the 23rd, Kershaw's men were ordered to strengthen the abatis in front of their lines. On November 30, Union information obtained from Confederate deserters had Kershaw moving towards Petersburg. On December 7, Kershaw received orders to replace General Hoke's Division. On December 10, they camped in front of Fort Harrison, Virginia. [13]

### Return To South Carolina/Conclusion

In January of 1865, rumors were abounding in Kershaw's Brigade about a transfer of some of South Carolina's troops to their home state to help " . . . swell the band that was at that time fighting on the flanks and front of Sherman." [14] During this time, while DuBose was in Virginia with Kershaw's Brigade, Sherman was following his infamous ride through Georgia in South Carolina and was in the process of devastating DuBose's home country. Destruction had been completed in Georgia and Sherman and his men were bound and determined to completely destroy South Carolina–the state where the war had begun.

When orders came for the remnants of Kershaw's Brigade to break camp and march for Richmond to be transported to South Carolina, the men were overjoyed. They were looking forward to fighting the invaders on home soil. On January 3, they were sent off to South Carolina aboard trains from Richmond. The order was that the brigade was being sent off "temporarily." [13] In his *Reminiscences*, DuBose makes a few comments regarding this journey:

> Soon after our return to Petersburg, we were ordered again to Charleston, South Carolina, and there we spent the brief time before the appearance in South Carolina of Sherman on his famous march. After passing through Columbia and Winnsboro, Sherman turned in the direction of Camden and Cheraw. At this later place the troops from Charleston were ordered to unite with the force which General Joe Johnston was gathering upon the trail of Sherman. As we left Charleston we marched through some of the haunts and homes of the Low Country . . . From there we marched to St. Stephen's—Here is the old Huguenot church where my grandfather is buried. I had never been at the old church. [7]

On February 16, Kershaw and generals Pickett and Benning received a communiqué from Assistant Adjutant-General Latrobe. It did not ask for a response, but requested the generals to consider something with discretion. The dispatch read:

> It is deemed desirable, and a request is made through General Lee, that the several corps of this army give an expression of opinion on the subject of putting Negroes, who for the boon of freedom would volunteer as soldiers, into the field. The effect of such a measure on this army is doubted, and consequently the matter is submitted to your discretion for obtaining the sense of your division on the subject. It may not be amiss to say that the opinion of the lieutenant-general commanding is that the adoption of

such a measure will involve the necessity of abolishing slavery entirely in the future, and that, too, without materially aiding us in the present. [13]

On the 17th of February, 1865, Sherman crossed the river to Columbia, South Carolina, by means of a pontoon bridge. He was met by the mayor, who asked that the city be protected. Sherman said his orders were to burn only military targets, but in spite of assurances, the entire city was virtually destroyed by fire. Sherman said that the Confederates did the burning; the Southerners insisted that Sherman's Army was guilty. Following the destruction of Columbia, Sherman moved on to Winnsboro on the 21st of February, where he continued the destruction. On March 12, 1865, a Union dispatch stated that Kershaw's and Pickett's divisions arrived at the Louisa Courthouse on March 9. [13]

On April 1-2, 1865, Kershaw's Brigade fought in the Battle of Five Forks. Stationed north of the James River, Kershaw's Division of the First Corps, with the garrison of Richmond and local defense troops, guarded fortifications. The infantry of the First Corps were under Kershaw. His troops, along with those of Custis Lee's, crossed the pontoon bridge below Richmond. The townspeople were in a frenzy because of the orders to evacuate. Because rioting and looting had broken out, Kershaw was ordered to hurry his troops to town. Although they were able to curtail the looting, fire became the larger problem. [13]

After the fights in the area of Petersburg, DuBose, with Kershaw's outfit was ordered to Charleston, South Carolina, to prepare for Sherman's march through that state. After they encountered Sherman, they followed him into North Carolina for two last-gasp skirmishes at Averasborough (March 16, 1865), and Bentonville (March 18, 1865). According to Dickert, there were 14,000 Confederates and 105,000 Yankees engaged at Bentonville, and, even at these final battles of the Confederacy, the men of Kershaw's

Brigade fought valiantly. The Northern losses were higher than the Southern and the Confederates captured nine hundred prisoners. [14] But once again, attrition prevailed–the Union was able to replace lost men, ammunition, and supplies but the South was not.

On April 6, 1865, came the finale of the Battle of Sayler's Creek. Three brigades of Kershaw's troops, under command of Ewell, formed into ranks and were placed as well as ground permitted. In front of them were low, scattered pine bushes for nearly 300 yards. The next obstacle was Sayler's Creek–not a formidable barrier. East of the stream was a cleared hillside leading up to a home. The Union infantry began its charge, but the four-year veterans of Kershaw fired at the oncoming Federals with a withering volley. However, the over-whelming numbers of the Federal troops turned the flank of Kershaw's right element.

Kershaw gave his troops as much direction as he could on the confused, fire-swept field. Within minutes, Kershaw, his staff, and all of the survivors of his Division, including Chaplain William P. DuBose, were captured. DuBose was in the hands of the Union troops for the second time during the four years of the war. Edwin Stanton, Union Secretary of War, sent a dispatch stating that on April 6, Sheridan attacked and routed General Lee's Army and he captured generals Kershaw, Ewell, Barton, Corse, and many others as well as thousands of prisoners and cannons. [13] Lee was expected to surrender any time, but Stanton said the telegraph was not working, so details were sketchy. Kershaw spent several months in prison after his capture at Sayler's Creek and then returned to South Carolina.

About April 26 in Greensboro, General Johnston surrendered according to terms agreed upon by Generals Lee and Grant at Appomattox. At that time $39,000 in silver, the last of the Confederate treasury, was received from the government in Richmond and divided among the soldiers. According to DuBose, his share came in handy as he returned home to begin rebuilding his area of his home state:

> . . . the cash in the Treasury of the Army at that time was
> distributed among the soldiers. My share was $1.50 in sil-
> ver. It was the first silver I had seen in a long time and it
> came in quite conveniently. My first expense was having
> my old war-horse, John, shod. I managed to procure and
> secure two mules, young mules, and with my servant,
> William, we started for home. Our only stop of any con-
> sequence was at Camden, of course with old friends
> there.[7]

According to military records at the South Carolina Archives in
Columbia, DuBose received his second and final parole from the
United States Government on May 1, 1865 (his first was received
after his capture at South Mountain in September, 1862). He left
Greensboro, North Carolina, where he was paroled, and headed for
South Carolina. His *Reminiscences* tell that his horse, John had sur-
vived the war.[7]

It is interesting that DuBose refers to "My servant, William."
What happened to Stephen, the body servant who first went to war
with William DuBose? He is not mentioned in the *Reminiscences*,
beyond early discussions when DuBose talked about their close relationship. Stephen was in poor health at the beginning of the war; perhaps DuBose had to send him home for replacement, much as he
sent home the aged horse, Archie. I find it interesting that DuBose
remembered the final disposition of his horse, but not his faithful servant, Stephen.

On May 24, 1865, DuBose was listed in the Annual Proceedings
of the Protestant Episcopal Church in South Carolina for the final
time as "The Reverend Wm. P. DuBose (deacon), Chaplain in the
Confederate Army."

DuBose said that the four years of the war were not a complete chasm in the midst of his preparation for his life's work. He had little opportunity for study or for progressive thought upon religious matters; yet, the time was not wasted:

> . . . the war did have its contribution to make, not only in its necessary effect upon my general as well as spiritual character, but more definitely in determining and strengthening my special bent. Having as adjutant always to carry along with me something of an office, with papers and books, and having also with me always a very faithful and devoted servant who took good care of myself and my belongings, I managed to carry a very few books all through the war. In time I secured an air-tight and very strong little ammunition box, which just held my books, and which, becoming well known, was always tossed into the headquarters wagon. In this box were five books, in English, Greek, Latin, and French- books that, in their contents as well as language, would not be exhausted or grow stale with constant use. Of these, those which are still with me are the Greek New Testament, Tennyson's "Poemes(sic)," Pascal's "Thoughts," and Xenophon's "Memorabilia. [6]

Although DuBose had little time for thoughts and study during the war, those moments he did find were ". . .sometimes more intense and precious, and probably more fruitful, for being so difficult and so in contrast with immediate avocation and environment." [7] During the war DuBose acquired a habit which stuck with him throughout his life as a theologian and teacher:

I acquired the habit of combining thought with life and experience: it is almost the case with me still that I am satisfactorily religious only in the act of thinking and studying, and successfully studious or thoughtful only as an act of religion. [7]

# Chapter VI

"The past cannot be recalled, and though it may
not soon be forgotten, yet it is the part
of Christian wisdom to bury it forever..."
— Presiding Northern Bishop
John Henry Hopkins

# AMERICAN RELIGION AND THE CIVIL WAR
## (1861-1865)

Charleston, downtown, circa 1865
LC

# CHAPTER VI

# AMERICAN RELIGION AND THE CIVIL WAR

## Synopsis

The Civil War and the defeat of the South had a serious impact upon the churches in that region. To understand the physical and spiritual condition of the church to which DuBose returned following the war, we must understand where the church was before and during the war.

Before the war the Protestant Episcopal Church, along with society in general, was undergoing internal upheavals, not the least of which were the impact of the Industrial Revolution and the place of slavery in a Christian Church. DuBose was raised the elitist son of a plantation owner and his participation in the war, both as soldier and chaplain, was made easier by the presence of his servant. So he had to come to grips with this dichotomy. The situation in South Carolina with a large number of freed, unemployed ex-slaves (approximately 50 percent of the population) was particularly critical. Also critical was the painful Reconstruction with its presence of Federal troops and the ever-present carpetbaggers and scalawags who made the loss to the Union that much more painful. The war had a great impact on all of the Protestant churches in the United States: most split before or during the war, some never to reunite. The Episcopal Church did separate during the war but managed to reunite fairly rapidly.

How did DuBose react to the loss of the South and the total restructuring of his personal and social existence? It might be said

that he ran away to join an 1870's Southern commune at The
University of the South–a commune that handled Reconstruction by
segregating its members from the outside world.  I cannot say yes or
no to this interpretation of his motives. The main thing that I can say,
as a 20th-century Episcopalian, is that I am glad he did escape to that
intellectual segregation that was The University of the South.
However, had he remained in parish life and work in South Carolina,
I am completely convinced that he would still have been a tremendous influence on the lives of many individuals.  Instead, by moving
to the University he had the stimulation, associations, and facilities
with which to proceed with studies and writings.  By these studies
and writings he helped make Christianity more personal and acceptable for those who followed him on the Episcopal path.

## Industrialization and Changes in American Religion

The new industrial way of life and its required factories affected American home life in other ways. They took men out of the home to serve as workers. They produced inexpensive goods that made home production techniques uneconomical. Instead of spinning yarn, weaving cloth, and making soap and candles and such at home, people now commonly bought these things at stores. DuBose talked about the self-sufficient nature of his boyhood plantation home. Little was purchased and most of what they needed was made at home. Married women were now left at home with many of their previous tasks no longer necessary and their previous skills no longer useful. The number of unmarried women grew drastically as the Civil War reduced the available young men. One man out of every fifty (620,000 men) died. As a consequence, many unmarried women entered the workplace

### The Episcopal Church Before the War

Rational orthodoxy was the mainstay of the Episcopal Church in the first third of the nineteenth century. By 1840 America was changing, and the rational approach to theology and the church no longer satisfied many Americans. The increase in industry in the north (e.g., textile factories in Lowell, Massachusetts, the Erie Canal, and the Baltimore and Ohio Railroad) told of a more sophisticated and industrialized nation. The triumph of an industrial North over an agricultural South in the Civil War made the picture clearer. This was no longer a frontier nation; the values of the nation and its people were different. Many Americans looked to religion to help them return to the "good old days," to create a closer connection with nature, cohesiveness of the frontier family structure, an awe of creation, and more spontaneity in life.

## The Episcopal Church

The American Revolution had a "liberating effect" on the religious life of the South, because the Church of England was disestablished after that war by most of the Southern States. Comparison of church memberships in the South prior to the war, principally in Virginia, North Carolina, South Carolina, and Georgia with a total population of about 3 million, was as follows:  99,000 Baptists, 94,000 Methodists, 23,000 Presbyterians, and fewer Episcopalians and Catholics. In South Carolina the overwhelming majority of the Up Country people were Baptist, Methodist, and Presbyterian. Churches such as the Episcopal Church, which were developed in an urban atmosphere or under the plantation system, did not appeal to the highly individual pioneers of the rugged Up Country. [43]

### The Episcopal Church in the United States

The Church of England was well established in Maryland, Virginia, North and South Carolina, and Georgia. However, the Baptist, Presbyterian and Methodist Protestant Churches had large numbers of members in these colonies, generally among those who were not plantation owners. The hard times that fell on the Church of England because of the Revolutionary War also came to the South after the Civil War and left the Protestants in control of the area.[41] The Anglican Church had been almost disestablished at the time of the Revolution but was reorganized after that war as the Episcopal Church of America.  But the Protestant Episcopal Church still thought of itself as the natural religious home for the region's socially elite. William E. Dodd stated this in the following terms: "Although there may be other roads to the Celestial City, no gentleman would choose any but the Episcopalian way.  It may be doubted whether there were twenty thousand Episcopalians in all the region from Charleston to Galveston at the outbreak of the Civil War, yet members of "the church" were almost invariably found in the seats of the mighty."[42]

The Church in South Carolina was, in effect, two churches–the Low Country (the tidewater, coastal plain, and the "Pee Dee" section), and the Up Country, a wild section sparsely settled by Scotch-Irish immigrants who came to this area from Virginia, Pennsylvania, and the North and brought with them their own religion, basically Protestant, simple, and fundamental. The Southern Anglicans established churches in the larger cities in South Carolina, as well as along the coast, in the Low Country. The emotional tone of the religion had been replaced by apathy, and the place of dominance was lost to religions of a more emotional and democratic nature. Most Episcopal pastors were emotional preachers.

Prior to the Civil War, the Episcopal Church had little success in operating colleges and seminaries in the South. The following had opened for a time but were all closed by the end of the war:  Madison College and Ravenscroft College in Tennessee, Kentucky Theological Seminary and Shelby College in Kentucky, St. Andrew's College and Rose Gates College in Mississippi, St. Paul's College and Wharton College in Texas, and St. Paul's College in Louisiana.  In addition, William and Mary University in Virginia, which had opened as an Episcopal facility, had become nonsectarian by 1865. [42]

Southern Episcopal bishops were interesting men and all were caught squarely on the horns of a dilemma–how to balance loyalties to country and to church.  All of the bishops, except for Bishop Johns, were of Southern birth and background and were from different parts of Virginia or the Carolinas. [22] They represented backgrounds of the wealthy plantation family, the poor farmer and the professional man, but all were distinctly Southern in moral and intellectual fibre, social habits, and prejudices.  Their attitudes toward slavery, division, and the right of a state to secede were representative of Southerners in general.

The Civil War was as much a blow to the Church as it was to the country.  During the war the Episcopal Church functioned independently in the North and South.  The Northern Church refused to recognize the separation, and the names of the absent Southern bishops were still called in the roll call of the General Convention in 1862. The Southern bishops did little more than organize an independent church, partly because of the difficulty of travel in the war-torn South. They did consecrate Richard Hooker Wilmer as Bishop of Alabama in 1862 and raised the status of Arkansas from a missionary district to a diocese in the Southern Church.

The Episcopal Churches of the North and South supported each other throughout the Civil War. During the war, the two regions of the country met in two separate bodies: the Protestant Episcopal Church in the United States of America and the General Council of the Confederate States of America. The Confederate Church was largely the result of efforts by Bishop Leonidas Polk of Louisiana and Bishop Stephen Elliot of Georgia. On March 23, 1861, Polk and Elliot addressed a circular letter to the bishops whose dioceses were in the Confederacy and proposed a convention to be held at Montgomery, Alabama, on July 3, 1861. At this convention it was resolved that the dioceses within the seceded states should form an independent organization.[22]

The Convention was attended by the bishops of Georgia, Mississippi, Florida, and South Carolina and by delegates from Alabama and Louisiana. The Convention reconvened in Trinity Church, Columbia, South Carolina, on October 16, 1861, and was attended by all the Southern bishops, except for Bishop/General Polk, who was with his command in the Confederate Army.

The Episcopal Church in South Carolina was in its annual meeting at Trinity Church in Abbeville shortly after the call to arms. Bishop Davis, when speaking to the Convention, spoke of the war in his address:

> Our hearth-stones are upturned. Our brothers and our children are in the field. Our youths with whom hitherto we have only sported have sprung up into armed men. We

are filled with deep emotions and trying expectations. But this is no time for weakness or fear. A country was never so saved. We are called upon for manly resolution and for Christian hope and trust. Our cause is right and our God is true. Let us show the world that we can trust both. Let us show them, too, that we are Southern men, and claim independent opinions and a sustaining individuality. We are not dependent upon circumstances or combinations or numbers for our inward strength, but can stand erect in personal character, in the sense of integrity and in the fear of God. [43]

Davis declared the Diocese of South Carolina a free and independent diocese. The Convention, at the end of the session of nine days, passed a motion written by the Rev. Dr. Wilmer;

*Resolved,* This Convention recommend to the several Dioceses within the Confederate States, until more permanent action can be taken, the provisional adoption of the body of Canons known as the "Canons of the Protestant Episcopal Church in the United States of America, so far as they are not in conflict with the political relations of the Confederate States, and do not interfere with the necessities of our condition. [22]

### Bishop/General Leonidas Polk–A Special Man

The presence of Bishop Leonidas Polk of Louisiana, a West Point graduate, might have made reunion difficult after the war. He was persuaded, (after refusing three times) by the early shortage of officers in the Southern Army, to serve; he proved to be an effective and beloved Confederate general. His death in battle in 1864 eliminated the possible question of his reinstatement. Polk played an important part in later discussions of The University of the South: he was one of the original founders of the institution. Bishop/General Polk was well thought of by the foot soldier. He is mentioned several times by Sam Watkins in his book *Co. Aytch*. During the Battle of Chickamauga, Tennessee, Watkins says: "General Leonidas Polk rides up and happening to stop in our front, some of the boys halloo out, 'Say, General, what command is that which is engaged now?' The General kindly answers, 'That is Longstreet's corps. He is driving them this way, and we will drive them that way, and crush them between the upper and nether millstone.' Turning to General Cheatham, he said, 'General move your division and attack at once.' Everything is at once set in motion, and General Cheatham, to give the boys a good send-off, says 'Forward boys, and give 'em h__l.' General Polk also says a good word, and that word was, 'Do as General Cheatham says, boys.' (You know he was a preacher and couldn't curse)."[16]

Watkins, who was present during the Battle of Pine Mountain when Bishop/General Polk was killed, spoke of his and all the other soldier's personal feelings for Polk in a testimonial to the General: "General Leonidas Polk, our old leader, whom we had followed all through that long war, had gone forward with some of his staff to the top of Pine Mountain, to reconnoiter, as far as was practicable, the position of the enemy in our front. While looking at them with his field glass, a solid shot from the Federal guns struck him on his left breast, passing through his body and through his heart. I saw him while the infirmary corps were bringing him off the field . . My pen and ability is inadequate to the task of doing his memory justice. Every private soldier loved him. Second to Stonewall Jackson, his loss was the greatest the South ever sustained. When I saw him there dead, I felt that I had lost a friend whom I had ever loved and respected, and that the South had lost one of her best and greatest Generals. His soldiers always loved and honored him. They called him 'Bishop Polk.' 'Bishop Polk' was ever a favorite with the army, and when any position was to be held, and it was known 'Bishop Polk' was there, we knew that 'all was well.'"[16]

A series of booklets for the Southern soldier, entitled *The Confederate Soldier's Packet Manuel of Devotions*, was prepared by the Reverent Charles Todd Quintard (later Bishop of Tennessee) and included a booklet for the chaplain, named *Balm for the Weary and Wounded*. The first four booklets off the press were forwarded to Bishop/General Polk in the field. Three of these copies were found in his breast pocket following his death and were stained with his blood. Polk had dated and signed the booklets over to three of his fellow generals whom he had baptized in the field, and they were forwarded to those men after his death.

Before the war Episcopalians had been an important part of the leadership of the South. In Southern cities their clergy were well educated and many Southern leaders, among them Robert E. Lee, were members of the denomination. Southern Episcopalians supported the Confederacy and enlisted in the armed forces. From North Carolina the Episcopal Church provided fifteen chaplains for the Confederate Army, and from Virginia it sent twenty-nine. From Georgia, six chaplains were furnished; from Mississippi five, from Tennessee three, from Louisiana and Texas two each, and from South Carolina, Florida, and Alabama one each. [22]

William Porcher DuBose is listed as the one commissioned chaplain from South Carolina and was attached to Kershaw's Brigade as Chaplain-at-large. [22] Jones, in *Christ in the Camp*, lists DuBose as Chaplain for "Brigade-at-large" for Kershaw's Old Brigade in Kershaw's Division, General Longstreet's First Corps. [44] The minutes of the 1863 Diocesan Convention state that " . . . all the students of the seminary had entered the military service of their country, all of which speaks well for the patriotism of the clergy."[45] The Episcopal Church sent many of her best priests as chaplains to the army, at least four of whom eventually became bishops (Quintard of Tennessee, Watson of East Carolina, Randolph of Virginia, and Gray of Florida).

### Reunion of the Episcopal Churches, North and South

The Episcopal Convention of 1865, following the conclusion of the war, was a crucial one because the Southern bishops were uncertain what kind of reception they would get when they attempted to return to the united church. Presiding Bishop John Henry Hopkins of the United States Episcopal Convention, a Vermonter, sent a letter to the separated bishops dated July 12, 1865, and made the invitation explicit: "I consider it a duty especially incumbent upon me, as the Presiding Bishop, to testify my affectionate attachment to those amongst my colleagues from whom I have been separated during those years of suffering and calamity; and to assure you personally of the cordial welcome which awaits you at our approaching General Convention. In this assurance, however, I pray you to believe that I do not stand alone. I have corresponded on the subject with the Bishops, and think myself authorized to state that they sympathize with me generally in the desire to see the fullest representation of churches from the South, and to greet their brethren in the Episcopate with the kindest feelings. The past cannot be recalled, and though it may not soon be forgotten, yet it is the part of Christian wisdom to bury it forever, rather than to suffer it to interfere with the present and the future interests of unity and peace."[22]

Two Southern bishops, Atkinson of North Carolina and his nephew Henry Lay of Arkansas, attended the Convention at the invitation of Presiding Bishop Hopkins. Atkinson, of all the Southern bishops, had been the least enthusiastic about the formation of a separate church. The two bishops were seated in the House of Bishops without question.[40]

The Convention accepted Bishop Wilmer's consecration and confirmed his position as Bishop of Alabama though at one point during the war, he, like many Southern bishops, instructed his parishioners not to pray for the President of the United States. Deputies from North Carolina, Texas, and Tennessee were present and seated in the House of Deputies. Some fire-eating Northerners tried to make trouble, but they were stopped. All went so well that no permanent breach occurred in the

Church, and at the next Convention the South was fully represented. In fact, by May, 1866, all of the Southern dioceses had indicated their wish to return to the General Convention.

Bishop Davis of South Carolina apparently clung to a hope that " . . . the Southern Church may be enabled to maintain her present and independent Catholic position," but by the time of the 1866 Convention, even he advocated an immediate return of the diocese into union with the Church in the United States. So, by 1866 the Church in the Confederate states ceased to be, and the Episcopal Church became the only major non-Roman body that was not permanently split by the Civil War.[43]

The war had distracted Episcopalians for some four years from the church party wrangling that had kept them busy from 1844 to 1860. When the war ended, it became obvious that the war had done more than disrupt the dispute: it had basically changed the character of the Episcopal Church. Among the Episcopalians the contest was perhaps more one of high church versus low church. Bishop John Henry Hobart of New York, the most outstanding figure on the high-church side, separated civic duty and religious responsibility. He tried to keep his church from secular campaigns, but his successors were not able to keep separate from a war that claimed parishioners and families. Many Episcopal churches in the North flew the American flag, and the House of Bishops began to issue pastoral letters endorsing the Union cause. Bishop Richard Channing Moore of Virginia and Bishop Philander Chase championed the cause of the low church. A split between factions was clear, and each election of succeeding bishops marked a new beginning of a campaign between the two factions of the Church. Slavery could hardly be called a factor in this in-house struggle. By war's end, Bishop Hobart's high-church philosophy was not acceptable.[41]

In the period before the Civil War the Church was growing pro-
portionately more rapidly than the population of the country. After
the war, although it continued to grow, the ratio of Episcopal Church
members to the population dropped. [41] This in part resulted from
the distress of the Church in the South after the war. Not only were
its buildings destroyed, but the plantation owners, its chief supporters, were impoverished. An even more telling reason was that the
growth of population in the United States in the latter part of the
nineteenth century was caused by vast numbers of immigrants. They
came to this country as members of some other church. Many of
their descendants, however, were eventually converted to the
Episcopal Church.

## Destruction of the Churches in the South

Defeat was a bitter pill to swallow for the Southerner and the chaplains, including William P. DuBose, returned home to a bankrupt, disheartened, and scattered people. Many churches in the South, particularly those in South Carolina and Georgia, had been located in the path of Sherman's march through the South. In the South five-hundred churches had been destroyed. The Presbyterians reported that between ninety and one-hundred of their churches had been destroyed. [35] Practically all of the church-supported colleges and universities closed their doors, and denominational administration ground to a halt. Sherman's troops had ulterior motives in mind other than the military goals of the march through South Carolina. The truth, according to Sherman, was that " . . . the whole army is burning with an insatiable desire to wreck vengeance upon South Carolina. I almost tremble at her fate, but feel that she deserves all that seems to be in store for her."

The Episcopal Church of South Carolina, to which William DuBose returned, was heavily damaged. DuBose was present at the Church's Annual Convention in 1868 as Assistant Secretary of the Convention. He was beginning to appear as a person on the rise in his home state's Episcopal Church.

*Impact of Sherman's March on the Episcopal Church in South Carolina*

Following is the report, "Committee to Collect Information Concerning Destruction of Churches and Church Property in the Diocese of South Carolina" in *The    Journal of the Proceedings of the 78th Annual Convention of the Protestant Episcopal Church in South Carolina*, St. Philip's Church, May 13-16, 1868: "The Committee to whom was referred the duty of gathering information with regard to the destruction of Churches and loss of Church Property during the war beg to Report: That they have discharged the trust committed to them as accurately as they could. It has required much patience and perseverance to obtain definite information as to the condition of many of the Churches which lay in the track of the invader. That fierce tornado which swept across our state from its southwestern to its north-eastern borders, leaving the ashes of cities, and villages, and Churches, and homesteads to mark its desolating track, so uprooted the foundations of our social and domestic life, as sometimes to leave few survivors to tell the tale. The destruction of railroads, the absence of postoffices, the loss of Church records, and the removal of those members of the congregation who were familiar with their parochial history, have often rendered it exceedingly difficult to obtain information authentic enough to embody in this report . . . To sum up the losses of the diocese, it appears: That ten Churches have been burnt; That three have disappeared; That twenty-two parishes are suspended; That eleven parsonages have been burnt; that every Church between the Savannah River and Charleston has been injured, some even stripped of weather-boarding and flooring; that almost every minister in that region of the State has lost home and library; that along the entire seaboard, from North Carolina to Georgia, where our Church has flourished for more than a century, there are but four parishes which maintain religious services; that not one, outside the city of Charleston, can be called a living, self-sustaining Parish; that their Clergy live by fishing, farming, and mechanical arts; and that almost every Church, whose history appears on this record, has lost its communion plate, often a massive and venerable set, the donation of an English or Colonial ancestor. Our Diocesan funds have shared the fate of all Southern investments. The Society for relief of the widows and orphans of the Clergy has lost $100,000. The Society for Advancement of Christianity in South Carolina has lost $56,000. Many of the older Churches also owned Bonds and Stocks, which have been sadly reduced or rendered worthless. From partial returns these losses amount to $98,000. The pecuniary losses might be repaired if the diocese was as in days gone by. But in its present impoverished condition, no hope remains of speedy restoration. This generation can scarcely behold it . . . "

### The War, Blacks, and The Episcopal Church

The number of black members of the Episcopal Church had been rapidly rising in the years preceding the Civil War, largely as a result of a concerted effort to minister to slaves in the South. Southern Episcopalians provided religious instruction for house servants who attended services with them, usually in separate balconies. During the 1840's and 1850's slave holders began an effort to evangelize agriculturally working slaves. Slave owners in lower South Carolina had constructed 100 plantation chapels. The number of black communicants rose from 489 in 1830 to 5828 in 1860.40 By 1860 black communicants were almost as numerous in the Diocese of South Carolina as whites. But, the Civil War ended slavery and at the same time ended the financial basis for new forms of evangelism: the plantation owners were impoverished.

The percentage of black Episcopalians fell in the years immediately following the war. In an effort to make an impact on this dwindling membership, the Episcopal Church created "Archdeaconries for Colored Work," and in Southern dioceses, clergy working in black parishes and the parishioners they served were placed in a pool from which black clergy could be drawn. This approach halted and appeared to reverse the decline in membership. However, white ambivalence about black membership and the gradual restriction of black participation in diocesan conventions, soon caused the decline to continue. [40]

Following the war, the majority of black Christians became members of their own independent bodies, such as the National Baptist Convention and the African Methodist Episcopal and African Methodist Episcopal Zion Churches. Some of the major white denominations had significant black minorities, and the number of black sects grew significantly, especially in metropolitan areas.

In *Chaplains in Gray* a case is made for the South in pushing the Civil War as primarily a matter of state's rights, rather than of slavery. [35] Norton, in *Rebel Religion* has the following to add to that:

> When, on the same day (April 19, 1861), he (Abraham Lincoln) announced his intention of invasion to force the return of the seceding states to the Federal Union, the patriotism of the South ran wild. The defense of homeland has long been held a sacred duty by men of all nations, and to this the clergyman of the South gave vigorous assent. To the typical Southerner, as to the typical Northerner, the freedom or servitude of the slave was not the paramount issue. There were many religious men in the South who deplored slavery and abhorred secession. Like one of their great leaders, Robert E. Lee, a man who was both anti-slavery and Unionist in sentiment, they found the postwar blanket indictment of all Southerners as defenders of slavery especially painful. True, they had defended the South, but they had done it as men who would not lift their swords against their own people. [34]

Some forty years following the war, William P. DuBose intellectually attempted to come to grips with the slavery issue and ultimate prohibition of slavery. He wrote:

> The world is constantly outgrowing and making sinful institutions which, however they are so now, were not so in the age or at the stage in which they prevailed . . . There are none of us now who do not sympathize with its (slavery's) extinction as a necessary step in the moral progress of the world. [6]

He went on to say:

It was natural that we who were in it and of it should be the last to see that, and be even made to see it against our will. Knowing as others could not, and loving the good that was in it, it was not strange that we should be more and longer than others blind to its evils, and unconscious of the judgment which the world was preparing, finally and forever, to pass upon it. Now that the judgment is passed, we join in it. Slavery, we say, is a sin, and a sin of which we could not possibly be guilty. [6]

DuBose further qualified his discussion by making a seemingly strange statement,

Little could we be guilty of charging with sin those who once nobly wore (slavery's) responsibilities and discharged its duties....Slavery in the South, at its best and in the person of its best, produced the largest, finest, and most delightful type of personal character that this country has ever known. [41]

---

### Impact of the War on Protestant Churches

The Civil War split the larger Protestant churches, because some of the Northern clergy were among the strongest advocates of the abolition of slavery. Except for the Methodists who have since reunited, the separation of most of the Protestant churches in the North and the South has persisted to the present time.

Most of the extensive, nineteenth-century Protestant denominational splits originally occurred in connection with the struggle over slavery. In 1843 the Wesleyan Methodist Church was formed because of the growing antipathy to slavery—the church was organized on the basis of no slave-holding members. This question was in the foreground in 1844 when the General Conference of the Methodist Episcopal Church met, and an immediate struggle arose over the retention of a slaveholding bishop. This Conference adopted a report that permitted the division of the church, and the Southern branch of that church, the Methodist Episcopal Church South, was constituted in 1845.[46]

The Baptists of North and South likewise split. The Alabama State Baptist Convention demanded in 1844 that the Foreign Missionary Board make no discrimination against slaveholders when deciding missionary appointments. The Board refused to make any statement implying approval of slavery, and the Southern Baptist Convention was formed in 1845.

As the Civil War drew nearer, other denominations divided. The Presbyterian Church split in 1857 (New School) and 1861 (Old School). The two southern wings reunited in 1864 as the Presbyterian Church in the United States, and the northern wings united in 1869-1870 as the Presbyterian Church in the United States of America.

# Chapter VII

"Sherman's march had swept the country clean..."
— W.P. DuBose

## THE PAIN OF RECONSTRUCTION
### (1865-1871)

Statehouse in Columbia, following Sherman's visit
LC

# CHAPTER VII

# THE PAIN OF RECONSTRUCTION

## Synopsis

In the five years between the end of the War and the time when DuBose made a change in his life to fulfill the philosophical and theological portions of the epitaph on his grave marker after his death, he became a rising star in the post-war Episcopal Church in South Carolina as he became active in the church at parish and diocesan levels. He was given two churches to rebuild, one of which had been totally destroyed and burned by Sherman's devastating march through South Carolina.

DuBose was named the assistant secretary of the annual Conventions of the Church, the body that administers the Episcopal Church. He was almost elected and named co-Bishop with Bishop Davis, an event that he later referred to as " . . . one of the most fortunate escapes of my life." [7] DuBose was saved from administrative duties and heavy paperwork that would have certainly cramped his creativity in the philosophical and theological arenas. However, the relative peace and quiet of the parish life had helped him again turn his sights toward study and reflection.

## Back To Carolina

In 1865 the war struggled on to its sad end, and following his second and final parole from the United States government, William DuBose found his way across the ravaged countryside to Winnsboro and then to Anderson to find his wife. On the trip back from North Carolina and thence through South Carolina, DuBose was still fulfilling his role as Chaplain to the Army, although no longer formally in that position. He mentions visits to widows of his fellow soldiers, where he had to go through the agony of describing specifics of their deaths on the battlefield. He says that "Widows and bereaved parents were at every turn, and worst of all, facing us everywhere was the loss of our country." [7]

DuBose discussed his trials in his attempt to get his wife back home from Anderson as follows:

> Sherman's march had swept the country clean of every facility for private travel, animals or vehicles, as well as provisions and everything else. Fortunately I had those two mules (author's note: the mules were those which DuBose had purchased with his Confederate severance pay), and fortunately there had been left an old barouche in which we children had once gone to school, but which had long been in disuse. For this we patched up what harness was just about sufficient for actual use (not for looks) and my man, William, myself, and my two little mules started across the state. [7]

DuBose's first concern was to get his bride home. He brought her to Farmington, where the problem, as on all plantations at that time, was to provide for the tremendous number of emancipated servants.

On October 1, 1865, the two Fairfield Episcopal churches, St. John's, Winnsboro, and St. Stephen's, Ridgeway, called DuBose from his impoverished plantation retreat to become rector. St. John's had been burned by Sherman's invading Federal troops, but fortunately, St. Stephen's was spared. Services in Winnsboro were held in the courthouse, as they had originally been before St. John's was built. On Bishop Davis' first visit a year later, he ordained DuBose to the priesthood, the next step in what was to be a life-time commitment for DuBose to minister to people.

Mr. and Mrs. DuBose returned to the desolation of Farmington Plantation, South Carolina. The town of Winnsboro was wrecked and burned; the presence of undisciplined troops, some of them black, added considerable confusion to the scene and led to demoralization of the people. The freed slaves, with no preparation for their freedom and no support from the government, were easily alienated and felt deceived. According to the Right Reverend Stephen Bayne, " . . . perhaps it is not to be wondered at that DuBose felt, as he said to his son, the condition of things compelled some such organization as the Ku Klux Klan." [8] I believe that in this case, DuBose was referring to the original Ku Klux Klan as a necessary police force, and not the hate-filled organization that evolved later.      Before the war the DuBose family had two large plantations, and DuBose agreed to go to Farmington, nine miles from town on very bad roads. He describes the situation as very bad, as the local blacks, whom DuBose described as before the war "having been one with ourselves," [7] now were forced to be very secretive with the DuBoses for their own protection. Farmington was also without animals, without farm implements, without seed, and without the capital needed to replace all of these and make the plantation usable again.

### Life in the Church Begins

While at Farmington, DuBose received a request from the Bishop to take St. John's church at Winnsboro. The church originally had been largely built by his father. A second small church in the area, St. Stephen's Mission of Ridgeway, was also to be handled by DuBose. St. John's Church building had been destroyed by Sherman's troops, and services were held in the county courthouse. A report of the specific damage caused to St. John's Church in Winnsboro was as follows:

> This Church was wantonly burnt by Sherman's troops, on their march through Winnsboro. The public square was destroyed, but the Church was not touched by that fire. It was on the outskirts of the town in a large lot, and was deliberately set on fire by the soldiers, after the central square was consumed. The organ, furniture, books, and all the Church property perished. It has involved a small congregation in a loss of $5,000. Their services are maintained, and there is some prospect of rebuilding the Church—the *only instance* in the diocese of any such proposal. [43]

Following his war experiences, DuBose rapidly became a rising star in the post-war Episcopal Church in South Carolina. When the Annual Convention met in Charleston on February 14, 1866, Wm. P. DuBose was listed as in charge of parishes at Winnsboro and Ridgeway and was "entitled to a seat and to votes except on matters affecting the temporal concerns of the churches." DuBose was also again named assistant secretary of the Convention.

DuBose was next called to be rector of St. John's, Fairfield, South Carolina, and on September 9, 1866, DuBose was ordained priest in the Episcopal Church by Bishop Davis. On October 15, 1866, the DuBose's first child, Susie Peronneau, was born. In the Proceedings of the 1867 Annual Convention, DuBose was listed as Rector of St. John's Church, Fairfield, South Carolina (founded in 1839), was still assistant secretary of the Convention, and "is now entitled to all privileges of members of this Convention."

DuBose maintained charge of these two church communities during 1866 and 1867. He also taught Greek at Mt. Zion College to make financial ends meet and to support his now growing family.

DuBose says that those two years were two of the most pleasant of his life, and he would have liked to have stayed longer to assist in the rebuilding of his home area. But on January 1, 1868, at the Bishop's request, DuBose took Trinity Church at Abbeville. According to him:

> . . . the church at Abbeville was one of the most beautiful in the state and the congregation and community one of the most distinguished. Abbeville had at one time been called the Athens of South Carolina . . . In my congregation there were a number of leading lawyers, judges, etc. [7]

On January 1,1868, DuBose's second child, May Peronneau, was born. In the Proceedings of the 78th Annual Convention of the Church, held at St. Philips Church in Charleston, on May 13-16, 1868, DuBose was listed as assistant secretary to the Convention and as Rector of Trinity Church in Abbeville, South Carolina. In the 1869 Proceedings of the Convention, held May 12-14, 1869 at St. Philips Church, DuBose is listed as assistant secretary of the Convention and as Rector at Trinity Church. He was actively involved in parish work as his annual report in the Proceedings shows;

## Trinity Church, Abbeville

### Rev. W.P. DuBose, Rector

| | |
|---|---|
| Baptisms, Infants 8, Adults 1 | 9 |
| Confirmed | 6 |
| Communicants, Admitted | 5 |
| Added by removal | 1 |
| Lost by removal | 3 |
| Died | 3 |
| Present Number | 51 |
| Non-communicants | 12 |
| Children under 14 | 37 |
| Families | 23 |
| Marriages | 2 |
| Burials | 4 |
| Children Catechized 12 times | 32 |
| Sunday School Teachers | 6 |
| Sunday School Scholars | 32 |

### Annual Budget

| | |
|---|---|
| Contributions, Communion, Alms | $97.00 |
| Salary | $600.00 |
| Other Parochial Objects | $46.25 |
| Missions,Diocesan | $120.00 |
| Domestic | $10.00 |
| Episcopate | $75.00 |
| Convention | $10.00 |
| Other Diocesan Objects | $65.00 |
| Total | $1,023.25 |

TABLE 3. LIFE IN THE CHURCH AT ABBEVILLE

Life in Abbeville was not calm and peaceful. The political climate there following the war during Reconstruction was bad. In an interesting parallel to Leonidas Polk, late bishop who had turned general, DuBose describes the situation of cleric turned warrior as follows:

> The carpet-bag regime was at its height and its worst. As elsewhere, there were in the community, besides the ordinary carpet-baggers, representatives known as scalawags, the former coming from abroad to reap benefits, but the latter being natives. The Negroes were influenced and became for a time very dangerous. Barns and sometimes dwellings were burned by night . . . Every citizen of the town was called upon to arm himself and take turns on night watch in the town. I had to buy a pistol and take my turn.[7]

During the 80th Annual Convention of the Church, held in Abbeville, May 12-14, 1870, DuBose remained assistant secretary to the Convention and was still listed as Rector, Trinity Church. On May 15, 1870, DuBose's uncle, Octavius Porcher, was ordained to the priesthood, and DuBose preached the sermon (published later as *The Christian Ministry*).[47] That same night, DuBose's first son, William Haskell, was born.

In June 1870, DuBose became even more prominent in the Episcopal Church in South Carolina as he joined the Reverend John DeWitt McCollough of Spartanburg in publishing a diocesan journal called *The Monthly Record*. The publication *replaced The Gospel Messenger* and the *Southern Episcopalian* and served more diocesan purposes than its two predecessors.[43] *The Monthly Record* contained many sketches of parishes. This publication continued until July, 1880, when it was replaced in turn by the *Church Herald*. DuBose was definitely beginning to show his bent for writing, a pastime that would remain with him for the remainder of his life.

In 1871, during the 81st Convention at Charleston, South
Carolina, DuBose was narrowly defeated (in 45 ballots) in the
election for assistant bishop. DuBose later commented that he was
glad he was not elected, because "I have always regarded this as one
of the most fortunate escapes of my life." [7] While church work in the
priesthood was to be his life, the administrative part of that calling
held no priority for him.

In the summer of 1871, DuBose received a telegram from The
University of the South, Tennessee, that determined the direction of
the rest of his life. It informed him that he had been elected Chaplain
of the University and Professor of Moral Science at The University of
the South in Sewanee. Another one of those surprise election/selec-
tions that DuBose seemed to attract. Now thirty-five years old,
DuBose began to wind up his parish-oriented activities at Abbeville
and prepare for what was to become his life's work. DuBose says that:

> The Board of Trustees was in session, and it was necessary
> to have an immediate reply. I had to make my decision
> without consultation with my Bishop, which was a great
> grief to me. I returned my acceptance, and prepared to
> make this change at the close of the year. [7]

In August of 1871, DuBose visited The University of the South
and acted in the position of chaplain for several months. From The
University of the South he attended the General Convention of the
Episcopal Church in Baltimore, Maryland. During that winter,
DuBose toured the State of South Carolina, discussing The
University of the South, and succeeded in taking a number of students to the school in March, 1872. He, with the cooperation of his
wife Nannie, spent the remainder of her inherited fortune in building Palmetto Hall at The University of the South. The building was
used as a dormitory for students from South Carolina for a number
of years.

In the published minutes of the 82nd Annual Convention of the Church, held in St. Philips Church, Charleston, DuBose was not listed as present. He was noted in the "assignments" as "Rev. Wm. P. DuBose, Professor and Chaplain in The University of the South." DuBose's formal work in local parishes in South Carolina was ended. However, he apparently visited his home state occasionally at Convention time, as a note in the Proceedings of the 1897 Council, which met in Grace Church, Anderson, stated that, "The presence was noted of the Rev. William P. DuBose, S.T.D., Dean of the Theological Department of The University of the South, and a warm greeting was extended to him." [43]

War and Reconstruction totally destroyed the South and its institutions–not just the industry or agriculture but the entire way of life. The world in which DuBose grew up no longer existed. The grace of a life built on the philosophies of the pre-war South was gone. The hope and dedication that moved the Confederacy was gone. There could be only the spirit of men like DuBose to give heart for the building that was to come. DuBose and the new world had to be created, and he had his part in it, in the community of The University of the South finding renewal and wholeness.

DuBose' role was to serve as teacher and in believing in what was to come. Through the years, years of ill health and poverty, the death of his first wife and the beginning of his second marriage, years of ceaseless work for The University of the South, he continually encouraged the new life within the University. He seemed to posses in his nature much of the spirit of his Huguenot ancestors who made their own new world in clearing the land and forming the plantations that had given life to the South Carolina area generations before.

# Chapter VIII

"Gentlemen, here is the spot, and here shall be the University."
— Bishop Leonidas Polk

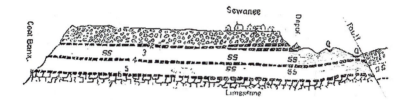

# SEWANEE YEARS
## (1871-1918)

Geologic Cross-section of the Sewanee, Tennessee area
Drawn by James Safford, 1893

# CHAPTER VIII

## SEWANEE YEARS (1871-1918)

### Synopsis

The University of the South in Sewanee, Tennessee, was a unique place. It was founded in pre-war times and even though the miniscule beginnings were destroyed during the course of the war, it somehow was recreated in post-war years in times when DuBose was excited to receive $1.50 from the Confederate Treasury as his share of the remaining silver. The life at post-war The University of the South was cheerfully described as community poverty, but it was an intellectual presence into which some of the greatest minds in the South retreated. On top of the mountain, one could almost forget that memories of the war and the current oppressive Reconstruction issues were much alive throughout the South.

DuBose threw himself into organization and disciplinary matters, building and expanding the university, forming the School of Theology, and most important of all, teaching. He had no intention of going into the writing and publishing game, but the prodding of his many devoted students to share his thoughts with the rest of the world forced him to do so, mostly in his later life. I would imagine that the details and rigors of writing, editing, and publishing were probably difficult for a man who, while teaching, would throw away his lecture notes from last year, so that he could begin with fresh thoughts and directions each school year. As a adjunct teacher for many years, I find this practice to be absolutely amazing.

As stated before in this book, I do not intend to go into the details of DuBose's theology, much of which has been described as difficult and hard to understand. Suffice it to say that modern theologians have found DuBose's work thoroughly modern, and ahead of his times. Most is relevant today.

DuBose himself once described his teaching method as well as how he eventually reluctantly became a published author:

> As my system and method of Exegesis grew and took shape in the thought and life of the class, questions naturally arose, and the newness of the presentation was often an irritation as well as a stimulant. I held that my place and part was <u>in the mine</u>, not <u>in the mint</u> of the truth of Christianity; that free inquiry and investigation, not dogma (which would have its proper place after) was in order with us. Everything was to be tested and verified, according to our Lord's prescription, in the light and in the terms of human nature, human life and human destiny. All that was true for us ought to be true to us. Questions that arose within the class began to spread without the class, and the time came when it became necessary to make known my teaching to a larger audience. I had no call or inclination to speak to the Church or the world save through my pupils, and it was they, not I, who in loving compulsion forced the publication of my first book, and have been behind, as well as in, all the rest. [6]

## The Humble Beginnings

The University of the South to which DuBose came had, like his homeland in South Carolina, been destroyed. The war and reconstruction laid a heavy hand on all of the southern institutions and on the way of life. The world in which DuBose grew up and which he loved was gone. The hope of the Confederacy was also gone, but men like DuBose nurtured hope for the building of what was to come. It was a new world in which DuBose found himself, and he had his part in the small community of The University of the South, finding there wholeness in the years to come.

### History of the Founding of The University of the South

It had long been the dream of Bishop Leonidas Polk that a great university should be established in the mountains of East Tennessee. He prepared a 4,000-word letter on July 1, 1856, to his brother bishops in the South and Southwest, stating that they were responsible for the spiritual well-being of all the people in those regions, regardless of their religious beliefs. On July 4, 1857, at Lookout Mountain, the nameless new institution began its existence. Bishop Otey, first Episcopal Bishop of Tennessee, gave the principal address. Among his words were these: "We affirm that our aim is eminently national and patriotic . . . not of political schism . . . We contemplate no strife, save a generous rivalry with our brethren, as who shall furnish to this great republic the truest men, the truest Christians, and the truest patriots." [48]

In the summer of 1857, a party consisting of John Armfield, V.K. Stevenson, John Bass, and Bishop Polk was accompanied by Dr. J.M. Safford, who went on to make a substantial name for himself in the geologic field. The group rode up Monteagle Mountain. The purpose of the trip was to determine if Sewanee was, indeed, the place for the university. Safford, later State Geologist of Tennessee and author of *The Geology of Tennessee* (1869), containing the first geologic map of the state, published memories of that ride up the mountain and Bishop Polk's excitement when he saw the present site of the university. The purpose of the trip was to examine the site's topography, geology, and mineral resources and to determine the possibility of water supply from several large springs. Safford's work was published in an 1893 Nomograph titled *Topography, Geology and Water Supply of Sewanee, Tennessee.* Safford reports that " . . . the Bishop rode over the ground, up one hill and down another, to this spring and to that until, reining up his horse in the midst of a beautiful growth of forest trees, and more than satisfied, exclaimed, 'Gentlemen, here is the spot, and here shall be the University.'" [49]

The Sewanee Mining Company made a grant of ten thousand acres to the school in 1858. According to the terms of the grant, the land would revert to the Mining Company if the school were not in operation within ten years. The State of Tennessee granted the charter for the fledgling university on January 6, 1858, and it was accepted by the trustees at their next meeting in July at Beersheba Springs. [42]

The first landscape gardener was Bishop John Henry Hopkins of Vermont, a multitalented man, skilled as an engineer, painter, musician, lawyer, and preacher. He took six months leave from his diocese, came to Sewanee in the fall of 1859 with Bishop Polk, and spent the winter. While there he drafted maps of roads and building sites and sketched two dozen water colors of scenes in the area. Unfortunately, during the war Yankee scavengers carried off most of the original water colors, and later efforts to find them were unsuccessful.

Part of the preparations for the grand opening included the hauling of a six-ton piece of variegated reddish-brown Tennessee marble up the mountain by means of oxen. The polished marble, which was to serve as the cornerstone, was laid on a wall of massive sandstone blocks set to support it. The bishops deposited in the stone a Bible, prayer book, copies of the constitution and the church canons, assorted other

Episcopalian papers, a church almanac, and unfortunately, several silver coins. Rumors of the "treasure" contained in the cornerstone prompted Federal soldiers to blow up the cornerstone and scatter the papers, records, and letters during the total destruction of the remaining buildings at the site. Fairbanks said, "The cornerstone, laid with such fond hopes, had been broken into fragments and its contents scattered beyond recovery, our humble buildings were in ashes, and the splendid endowment, secured with such toil and effort, had vanished. Otey, the noble, great-minded chancellor, and Polk, the moving spirit of the enterprise, were in their graves, and the University and its grand ideal seemed to have left behind only a sweet memory of a great name." [50]

In 1859 the large springs and prominent points present in the topography of The University of the South were named by Bishop Green and Rev. Fairbanks in honor of the early friends, benefactors, and founders of the University. The large spring near Tremlett Hall was named Polk's Spring; the one in the rear of A.T.O. Hall became Otey Spring; and others included Green's Spring, Cobb's Spring, Green's View, Croom's Bluff, Morgan's Steep, and Point Rutledge. [50]

After the Battle of Murfreesboro the Confederate Army under General Bragg had fallen back to Tullahoma, then crossed the mountain at Sewanee. In an ironic twist, General/Bishop Polk, while involved in fighting with Bragg in July, 1863, retreated with his forces over Sewanee Mountain; he must have been sorely depressed when he saw the destruction there. Several detachments of Federal troops later camped at Sewanee for long periods of time, and all the houses were burned. No further fighting occurred in that area, and underbrush eventually covered the entire site.

Following the war, there was every chance that the University would violate the "ten years clause" in the original land grant from the Sewanee Mining Company and lose the property. So, the newly named Bishop of Tennessee, Charles Todd Quintard, former chaplain of the First

Tennessee Confederate Regiment, moved quickly. He visited the site, climbed the hills, and marked spots for new buildings to replace those that the Northern troops had destroyed during the war. Quintard traveled to England and made a good case to the English people: he received substantial financial support for the founding of the university, along with handsome collections of books to begin the library.[50]

The University had been founded on the premise that southern sons needed a central institution because too often in the past the sons of planters had been sent north to school. In this school, "the sons of Southern planters could be protected from Northern radicalism and could freely drink pure and invigorating draughts from unpolluted fountains.[50]

This new institution was visualized as a way by which the South could be brought together as a nation. The school calendar was adapted to the pre-war conditions of Southern life. The students were to be at school during summer months, when there was nothing for them to do at home save get into trouble, but they received a long Christmas vacation, when the sports that were preeminent in the South could be pursued.

In September, 1868, The University of the South reopened. The three principal administrators and more than half of the faculty were former Confederate officers. According to Charles E. Thomas in an article in December 28, 1958, issue of the Columbia, South Carolina newspaper, *The State*, when The University of the South reopened in 1868, General Robert E. Lee was invited to be vice-chancellor, but he turned the post down with a letter that stated that he had just accepted the presidency of "another small college," (now Washington and Lee University). Lee did recommend General Josiah Gorgas, well known because of the incredible job he did as chief ordnance "scavenger." Gorgas accepted the post as vice-chancellor of the University.

## The Arrival of DuBose

William Porcher DuBose completed one and-one-half years at a South Carolinian diocesan seminary prior to 1861 and the firing on Fort Sumter and his active participation in the Civil War. This seminary had only a brief existence. It was founded by Bishop Davis and, after being interrupted by the Civil War, was moved to Spartanburg in 1868, where it survived only briefly because of poverty and because of the church's greater interest in The University of the South. These one and one-half years were his total formal religious education. This limited formal training might have been a handicap for most people, but certainly was not for William DuBose.

On July 17, 1871, DuBose was elected Chaplain of The University of the South and he served in that post until July 30, 1883. He was invited to become Professor of Moral Philosophy, and he never left that post: he served until his retirement. One person who was at least partially responsible for DuBose's invitation to the university was Major General Joseph Brevard Kershaw. A distant relative of DuBose's, he was part of the successful effort to remove DuBose from the active firing line during the war and was the officer in charge of the troops that DuBose served as chaplain for the last two war years.

Before he left home for the long trip to The University of the South, DuBose made a recruiting trip throughout South Carolina. In the past, only two students from South Carolina had come to the university, but DuBose was a successful recruiter: twenty-four new students made the trip back to school with him. His recruits made up ten percent of 1871's student body. DuBose's home became an oasis for the students. Dances were held in his dining room, penny readings in the parlor, and ice-cream parties outside on the lawn. [42] DuBose encouraged training in character, conduct, and dress and considered such training as important as learning. He promoted the wearing of coat and tie to class as being the sign of a gentleman.

During the winter of 1876-77, DuBose and Rev. J.A. Van Hoose made a special effort to secure funds for the endowment of a chair in the theological department; they collected $2,200.[50] DuBose was one of the founders and second dean of the School of Theology in 1878. He wrote seven books and numerous articles that reveal a profound theological mind. He is appreciated as a theologian more in England than by his fellow Americans (because of a prejudice that still lingers in this country against Southern scholarship?). The Preparatory Department opened in 1868, the college in 1870, and the Theological School in 1880.

DuBose's beginning at The University of the South included surrounding himself with family members. His brother, Robert, and his brother's wife, Mrs. McNeely DuBose, took charge of Palmetto Hall, and his cousin, Miss Maria Porcher, built Magnolia Hall on the adjoining lot. Before DuBose could build his home and bring his family, he lived with General and Mrs. Gorgas. Gorgas was the vice-chancellor of the Institution and was in charge of and responsible for the military character of the school. In 1871 the change was made to develop the school as a University atmosphere rather than as a military environment, and DuBose said that "this was a difficult process, and was for some years a source of trouble." [7] DuBose had been given the task of converting the atmosphere, and in this endeavor he proved to be gentle but firm as an administrator and disciplinarian.

Bishop/General Polk had predicted that The University of the South would create its own society, and it did just that. The three dozen families of teachers and administrators living within a few hundred yards of the chapel were a close-knit group. They had a number of synergisms, including family ties, religion, poverty, the Southern cause, and well-developed scientific, cultural, and literary ties. All the families encouraged community ties through activities that included entertainment, concerts, and student activities. The school featured all that was good in the aristocratic influence of the Old South. The university became a retreat for hopes and dreams of

Southern society. It remains so today: many members of the boards and some residents are descendants of the founding fathers.

The church and The University of the South at Sewanee became DuBose's life. The church became the channel through which he continued to express his loyalty to the South and his beliefs in the values of the plantation elite.

In the Fall of 1872, the DuBose's fourth child, Samuel was born. In April, 1873, Mrs. Anne Barnwell DuBose died, followed by Samuel in the spring of 1874.

In 1877, the Theological Department was listed in the University's Proceedings as a separate school, and DuBose was listed as Professor of Hebrew, Exegesis and Homiletics. On December 1878, DuBose married Maria Louise Yerger. In 1886, the strain of starting the School of Theology proved to be too much for the fragile health of DuBose, and he contacted tuberculosis at the age of fifty. The The University of the South community contributed a remarkable purse, considering the poverty of the faculty and staff. They sent DuBose on a trip to recover his health. The trip included Niagara Falls, The Philadelphia Centennial, and the Cincinnati Zoo, where DuBose was reported to have been delighted at the antics of the monkeys in the cages.

The second Mrs. DuBose died in 1887. In 1892 DuBose published *Soteriology of the New Testament.* [51] In September of 1893, DuBose was named acting dean; on July 31, 1894 , he was elected dean by the trustees. In 1896 DuBose published *The Ecumenical Councils* (Volume III *of Ten Epochs of Church History,* by John Fulton) [52]; in 1906 *The Gospel in the Gospels* [53] and in 1907, *The Gospel According to St. Paul.* [54] From 1907 to 1908, DuBose served as lecturer at General Theological Seminary. His lectures were published as *High Priesthood and Sacrifice* [5] In 1911 he published *The Reason of Life,*56 and in 1912, *Turning Points in My Life.* [6] From 1913 to 1920

he published eleven articles in The Constructive Quarterly; the articles were re-published in 1957 under the title *Unity in the Faith*.

DuBose created his Memoirs (*Reminiscences*) [7], later transcribed
by his son, William Haskell DuBose, during the period of his retirement. The *Reminiscences* were never published, but have been
extremely helpful to all who have written of DuBose since then,
including the present writer. The *Reminiscences* were informally told
to his daughters and their friends, and taken down by one of the
friends. DuBose never edited the *Reminiscences*, but as Bratton said,
and as I have found to be true also, the details of them are so accurate that they are quite usable in research. They are casual in nature
and not up to the standard of writing of his many publications but
are quite delightful in their existing form.

Photographs included in the present book are reproduced by
permission of the Archives of The University of the South. One thing
I noticed very clearly in every one of the photographs, from the
beginnings of the Civil War through to his death in 1918, is the
piercing eyes of William DuBose–they never changed.

DuBose's life evokes the images of a culture that was oppressive
and narrow. He lived in a world clinging to the cultural ideals of a
South whose values seemed to be a combination of the novels of Sir
Walter Scott and a plantation economy. As perceptively summarized
by Urban Holmes, "William Porcher DuBose is probably the most
original theologian the Episcopal Church has produced. I also find
him something of a fascinating enigma". [3]

The world of DuBose was definitely both racist and sexist, both
before and after the Civil War. Blacks were not allowed at the university and were considered to be servants chosen by divine providence. DuBose was tended until his death by his two unmarried
daughters, and everyone seemed to think that this was an appropriate sacrifice on their part.

On August 18, 1918, DuBose died in Sewanee at 82 years of age. Bishop Mikell of Atlanta, a former pupil, gave him his last sacrament. DuBose, ever the teacher and comforter to the last, said to his children around his bedside, "You need not think that I have not been thinking of death. I have been looking at it from all sides. I have looked death in the face, and felt it in my body, and I am ready to meet it. If God should take me tonight I would be glad. The Eternal Father, the risen Christ, the Blessed Holy Ghost have been my companions." [2] In 1970, DuBose was added to the Liturgical Calendar of the Episcopal Church as a modern-day saint.

DuBose's Alma Mater, The Citadel, counts him as one of their shining stars of achievement. DuBose is listed in three places in Thomas.[56] He is called "prominent among these shining examples of the best products of the school may be mentioned". DuBose's detailed life history in Thomas reads as follows:

> William Porcher DuBose, M.A., S.T.D., gallant soldier of the late war; learned Professor; scholar and model Divine, pure in thought and life; as author of "The Socteriology of the New Testament–a recent work–pronounced by an eminent Divine of the North one of the greatest Theologians of America. [56]

In a listing of the graduates of The Citadel 1842-1865, DuBose's name is marked with an asterisk, indicating that he graduated with highest honors in his class of 1855. His complete biography is given as follows;

> W.P. DuBose, Fairfield District, 1855; Degree of M.A., University of Virginia, '63; Student Theology. Seminary of the P.E. Church, Camden, S.C., 1859-'61; Adjt. Holcombe Legion, 1861-'64, severely wounded several times and prisoner in Ft. Delaware; Chaplaincy of Kershaw's Brigade, 1864-'65; said Chaplain appt. made

without his cooperation or knowledge; Pastor St. John's
Ch., Winnsboro, S.C., 1865-'68; Do. of Trinity Ch.,
Abbeville, S.C., 1868-'71; Chaplain and Prof. Ethics,
University of the South, 1871-'80; Resigned Chaplaincy
and took chair of Exegesis in Theol. Dept., 1880; Recd. in
1875 the honorary degree of S.T.D. from Columbia
College, N.Y. [56]

# Chapter IX

"William Porcher DuBose is probably the most original theologian
the Episcopal Church has produced. I also find him
something of a fascinating enigma."
— Urban T. Holmes

# THEOLOGY OF DUBOSE

Portrait of W.P. DuBose near end of teaching career (circa 1905)
Courtesey The University of the South Archives

## CHAPTER IX

## THEOLOGY OF DUBOSE

Synopsis

Something in the The University of the South life and in the theology of William Porcher DuBose seemed to have been pulled from the traumatic experiences of the war. At the time of his death in 1918, Bishop Guerry quotes a reviewer who wrote that: "The atmosphere of the battlefield is still potent in (his) theology. Sometimes he reaches the height of his argument by what may seem a flanking movement and a circuitous route. But he never loses sight of his destination . . . " [1]

Bishop Guerry appeared to at least partially agree with this statement, and he goes on to comment about his own assessment of "the military in DuBose's character":

However fanciful that may be as a comment on his theology, it is certainly true that the lessons of the war were not lost in DuBose. His utter courage in declaring truth as he saw it, the deep sense of comradeship with his students, his honesty in accessing the real situation— whether in theological argument or in a practical program for Sewanee— these are military virtues. [1]

DuBose, in *Turning Points of My Life*, discussed in detail the impact that his service in the military, the solitary meditations, and the accompanying scarcity of books for the four years of the war had on his study and his thoughts:

The solitary habit of thinking out such thoughts and living out such life as came to or grew up in me in the four
years of active military service, interspersed with trying
adventures, wounds, imprisonment, and deeper experiences even than these, away from all help of teachers or
books, cannot of course but have modified and fixed my
mental habits and bent. I would not have it supposed that
on my return to the wide world of outside life and
thought, from which we had been so long shut out, I did
not put myself at school to it, and have not desired to keep
myself in touch with the learning and the movements of
my time. I had learned to live too much, no doubt, in my
own thinking, and have made great use of, perhaps, too
few helps. But there are compensating benefits: one is, I
think, that I can never use a commentary, or seek a help of
any kind, unless or until I thoroughly need and want
it–that is, until I have done all that I possibly can with the
matter myself. I even try too much to be my own dictio-
nary and grammar. [6]

## Philosophy of DuBose

Bratton says of DuBose's philosophy that

> he has given to the world the most significant contribution
> to the Philosophy of Christians which has been made in
> our modern age. It is also because his philosophy presents
> an enduring vehicle of truth, of universal application to
> the expression of the truth and its molding power in
> thought and life. [2]

William DuBose rejected any belief that Scripture was a revelation of knowledge or doctrine, and he wrote as follows:

> The New Testament assumes the truth of Christ and of
> human salvation in Christ; it does not create or originally
> communicate this truth. It nowhere professes to be a primary or original revelation of the facts or truths of
> Christianity or a final statement of Christian doctrine.
> Rather, it presupposes the truth as having being revealed in
> Christ and already existing in the mind of the Church. [57]

DuBose also expressed his interpretation of freedom. He said, "The will that has not power, that is not free, to obey its true law, is in bondage to some false law. Morality is the only freedom. Anything else is slavery." [7]

The Incarnation was central to DuBose. In words similar to an early theologian of the Christian Church, Irenaeus (130-200), he wrote, "I see in Jesus not only the supreme act of humility in God, but the supreme act of humanity in God." [57] He saw in our Lord a human nature more human than our own. He spoke of this in terms of breadth and depth.

Life was for DuBose most precious–everything we do, he says, is for life–not the other way around–and life is most manifest in Christ.

The understanding of the play of light and darkness within creation and God himself is important if we are to embrace the Incarnation for what it can mean. DuBose was one who had seen the horror of war, he had experienced the death of many whom he loved, and he lived in virtual poverty. Yet he could still say that God is life, this life which sometimes appeared so evil. In fact, it seemed that, in the very acknowledgment of that evil grace flowed into his mind and heart. This is a mystery, but so is the Incarnation. [57]

DuBose was known as a genius in his teaching. Bishop Manning, who was first student and then colleague of DuBose, described DuBose's teaching this way:

> His teaching meant to those who followed it not a mere intellectual apprehension, but personal, spiritual conviction and experience. It brought home to them the actual reality of the Gospel, the stupendous truth of the Incarnation, and the fact that Christianity means faith in our Lord Himself as a Person, with a power which could never be forgotten.

DuBose seemed to wrestle with the concreteness of Christian life in a paper to the Fifth Church Congress:

> The Episcopal Church's claim to be a catholic church must mean only this and nothing more, that we desire and intend and believe ourselves to be within all the essential and necessary principles of the catholic faith, life and worship, of the one Church of Christ–This meant that the Episcopalians must be turning their face toward the theory of the one church of Christ and moving in the direction of it. [6]

William Porcher DuBose is, perhaps, the most important theologian the "godfilled South" has ever produced. [58] His works were reviewed in journals published all over Europe and, later, in the

United States. The theologians were and are almost unanimous in praise of his work. Following are a few of the comments that have been published about his theology:

> William Porcher DuBose is probably the most original theologian the Episcopal Church has produced. I also find him something of a fascinating enigma. [3]

> Above all, Christianity is an extraordinary living thing in his books. [59]

> America should make much of Dr. DuBose. I strongly suspect that in his own proper field . . . he is the wisest writer on the other side of the Atlantic; indeed it may not be too much to say, the wisest Anglican writer . . . on both sides of the Atlantic. [60]

> William Porcher DuBose was the only important creative theologian that the Episcopal Church in the United States has produced. [61]

> In the Episcopal Church, William P. DuBose of the Sewanee Seminary (Tennessee) was probably his church's greatest theological mind. No Southerner of his period equaled his richness and depth of thought, yet his moderate, tradition-oriented liberalism was not widely noted, possibly because Catholic-Evangelical conflict consumed so much Episcopal energy. [62]

How did William Porcher DuBose see his religious odyssey when it was close to completion? His view was best told in a letter to his old friend and former student, Silas McBee, in 1916, when DuBose was eighty years old, and, I think, shows his life-long relationship with St. Paul:

In a sense this eightieth year of my life has been one of worse than European War between me and old age.  In this I feel that I can say modestly that I have conquered . . . it has only had the beneficent effect, as most certainly the gracious purpose, of throwing me back upon a re-examination and a deeper questioning and testing of my religion. I have gone deeper into it, and reached higher than ever before, and I humbly believe I can say now "I not only believe but know." At any rate, I have discovered that the more persistently and perseveringly one believes to the bitterest end, the more certainly one knows, and is grateful for having been spared none of the tests . . . I have nothing to show, but I am firmer on the rock.

# Chapter X

"I have nothing to show, but I am firmer on the rock."
– W.P. DuBose

# CONCLUSIONS

Dean Emeritus W.P.DuBose during DuBose Reunion week at
The University of the South (August 1-6, 1911)
Courtesy The University of the South Archives

# CHAPTER X

# CONCLUSIONS

The question I asked when I began this biography was whether William Porcher DuBose was a racist, sexist, and elitist person by choice or personality, or whether he had these traits because he was the epitome of a product of his times. The attitudes of the 1990's truly makes any of these three personality traits unacceptable in society. Should a modern Episcopalian feel somewhat nervous to realize that a modern day saint on the church's calendar could have been "guilty" of these attitudes and opinions?

I have formed my own opinions as to the answer to this question, based on the reading I have done on everything written about or by William DuBose. I would like to give my opinions separately about each personality trait.

**Racist?** I do not believe that you could call DuBose a racist in the true sense of the word. He certainly never went so far as to become an abolitionist, but in his later life, he lived and associated with the blacks that lived and worked at The University of the South. We must remember that DuBose was born and raised in a society that barely recognized blacks as human and certainly not as the equal of the white man.

DuBose thought a great deal about this, and made his definitive statement as to how he felt about racism: "Slavery, we say, is a sin, and a sin of which we could not possibly be guilty." [6] In other words, the institution of slavery he recognized for what it was–an evil. However, he did not believe that the individuals involved in slavery as a way of life, until such time the institution of slavery was damned as evil, were themselves sinners.

**Sexist?** Once again, the times were certainly sexist. Women were to stay at home, keep house, have babies, and wait on their husbands. Was DuBose a sexist? Undoubtedly, he was, but I offer one interesting thought. After his first wife, Nanny, died in 1873, DuBose remarried in 1878, to Maria Louise Yerger. Mrs. Yerger, before her marriage to William DuBose, was a successful schoolmistress. I doubt that DuBose could have remained a total sexist, being married to a successful woman of the times.

**Elitist?** In his early life, through the end of the Civil War, William DuBose was certainly an elitist. He was born and raised and educated in a society that was based on elitism—the plantation owners and their offspring considered themselves as the nearest thing to royalty in the United States of America. The Southern "caste system" was based on European society, which was also certainly elitist in nature. However, this was a trait that undoubtedly changed substantially when DuBose joined the faculty and the community at The University of the South at Sewanee. He committed himself to a life of poverty, "cheerful poverty," as DuBose himself called it.[7] If he remained an elitist, it would only have been an intellectual elitist, as a faculty member in an institution with excellent academics. Perhaps he could be more easily forgiven as an academic elitist than as an elitist on the basis of birth or position or rank or family background.

Was William DuBose an elitist theologian up in his ivory tower spouting forth theology? I think not. He was coerced to begin his writing by former students and his bishop only very late in his life. DuBose was a teacher who destroyed his notes from the previous year so that he could begin each new year fresh. This doesn't sound like an elitist who hangs on every one of his own utterances, but a man who thoroughly enjoyed the interactions with a fresh set of students who had their own ideas. He was also a man whose home was open to students for discussions and relaxations, and the students took advantage of the opportunity, and gathered there in large numbers.

I believe that one deep insight to DuBose's mind and character and his personal Christianity and relationship to family and friends was in the *Reminiscences*, in his poignant description of the death of his infant son, Samuel.

> The little Samuel throve and grew and was unusually well and strong, but in the spring of 1874–He was fond of playing. Every night the four children used to play in the parlor. He would come in with his long nightgown tucked up so he could walk and he was devoted to a little play I had— But in the spring of '74, he had a severe bronchial attack and lost his voice entirely. He lingered and lingered. I used to carry him in my arms and he loved it. He died. I miss that little boy to this day. I miss him <u>now</u>. Dear little fellow! <u>Dear</u> little fellow!——(No more tonight.) [7]

So, in conclusion, William DuBose, soldier, theologian, and philosopher in life and saint after his death, was raised and educated to be racist, sexist, and elitist. He was definitely the enigma that Urban T. Holmes branded him. However, I believe his writings show that he grew far beyond these early inherited tendencies to become the theologian named by his contemporaries and those doctors of the church who followed him as the most important ever in the Episcopal Church in the United States.

Plate 4
W.P. DuBose, early in career (circa 1875)
Courtesy The University of the South Archives

Plate 5
W.P. DuBose midway in career (circa 1890)
Courtesy The University of the South Archives

Plate 6
W.P. DuBose late in career (circa 1905)
Courtesy The University of the South Archives

Plate 7
Dean Emeritus W.P. DuBose during DuBose Reunion Week, August 1-6, 1911
Courtesy The University of the South Archives

Plate 8
W.P. DuBose with grandson during DuBose Reunion Week, August 1-6, 1911
Courtesy The University of the South Archives

Plate 9
Dean Emeritus W.P. DuBose during DuBose Reunion Week, August 1-6, 1911
Courtesy The University of the South Archives

## WORKS CITED

1 Guerry, Moultrie. *Men Who Made Sewanee.* Sewanee, Tennessee: University Press, 1932.

2 Bratton, Theodore DuBose. *An Apostle of Reality: The Life and Thoughts of the Reverend William Porcher DuBose.* A Series of Lectures on the DuBose Foundation Delivered at The University of the South. New York, New York: Longmans, Green and Co., 1936.

3 Holmes, Urban T. *What is Anglicanism?* Harrisburg, Pennsylvania: Moorehouse Press, 1982.

4 Evans, General Clement A. *Confederate Military History, Vol. V, South Carolina.* Atlanta, Georgia: Confederate Publishing Company, 1899.

5 DuBose, William Porcher. *The Reason of Life.* New York, New York: Longman's, Green, and Co., 1911.

6 DuBose, William Porcher. *Turning Points of My Life.* New York, New York: Longman's, Green, and Co., 1912.

7 DuBose, William Porcher. *The Reminiscences of William Porcher DuBose, D.D., ST.D..* Sewanee, Tennessee: Unpublished, compiled by William Haskell DuBose, typed copy lent to the University of North Carolina by Mrs. Joseph M. Bell, circa 1911.

8 Bayne, Stephen F. *In the Mine, Not the Mint; A Sketch of the Life of William Porcher DuBose.* New York, New York: St. Luke's Journal, XV, 4, September, 1972, The Blue and The Gray Press, Distributors, 1972.

9 Chesnut, Mary (editor, C. Vann Woodward). *Mary Chesnut's Civil War.* New York, New York: Book-of-The-Month Club, 1981.

10 McPherson, James M. *Battle Cry of Freedom.* New York, New York: Oxford University Press, 1988.

11 Angle, Paul M. *A Pictorial History of the Civil War Years.* New York, New York: Nelson Doubleday, Inc., 1967.

12 Romero, Sidney J. *Religion in the Rebel Ranks.* Lanham, Maryland: University Press of America, Inc., 1983.

13 Scott, Robert M. *The War of the Rebellion: A Compilation of the Official Records of the Union and Confederate Armies.* Washington, D.C.: United States Government Printing Office, 1880 (first vol.–subsequent volumes published through 1895).

14 Dickert, D. Augustus. *History of Kershaw's Brigade (with Complete

*Roll of Companies, Biographical Sketches, Incidents, Anecdotes, Etc.).* Dayton, Ohio: Press of Morningside Bookshop, 1973 (original, 1899).

15 Stern, Philip Van Doren. *Soldier Life in the Union and Confederate Armies.* New York, New York: Bonanza Books, 1961.

16 Watkins, Samuel Rush. *Co. Aytch, Maury Grays, First Tennessee Regiment.* Dayton, Ohio: Morningside Bookshop, 1982.

17 Wiley, Bell Irvin. *The Life of Johnny Reb–The Common Soldier of the Confederacy.* Indianapolis, Indiana: Charter Books, Bobbs-Merrill Company, 1943.

18 Jones, Archer. *Civil War Command and Strategy: The Process of Victory and Defeat.* New York, New York: The Free Press Division of Macmillan, Inc., 1992.

19 Thompson, David L., Company G, 9th New York Volunteers, in Bradford,1956

20 Amann, William Frayne. *Personnel of the Civil War.* New York, New York: Thomas Yoseloff Publishers, 1961.

21 Baker, Gary R. *Cadets in Gray: The Story of the Cadets of the South Carolina Military Academy and the Cadet Rangers in the Civil War.* Columbia, South Carolina: Palmetto Bookworks, 1989.

22 Cheshire, Joseph Blount. *The Church in the Confederate States.* New York, New York: Longmans, Green, and Co., 1912.

23 Pollard, Edward A. *Southern History of the War.* New York, New York: The Fairfax Press, Crown Publishers, 1866.

24 Winchester, Kenneth, editor. *Brother Against Brother, Time-Life History of the Civil War.* New York, New York: Prentice-Hall Press, 1990.

25 Ropes, John Codman. *The Army Under Pope.* New York, New York: Jack Brussel, Publisher, 1880(?).

26 Pollard, Edward A. *The Lost Cause; A New Southern History of the War of the Confederates.* New York, New York: E.B. Treat and Company Publishers, 1867.

27 Eisenschiml, Otto, and Ralph Newman. *The Civil War: Volume 1: The American Iliad as told by those who lived it.* New York, New York: Grosset & Dunlap, Inc., 1956.

28 Gaillard, Franklin, Fred E. Gaillard, editor. *Civil War Letters.* Sewanee, Tennessee: n.p., 1941.

29 Keiley, A. M. *In Vinculis, or, The Prisoner of War.* New York, New York. 1866.

30 Ward, Geoffrey C. *The Civil War: An Illustrated History.* New York: Alfred A. Knopf, New York, 1990.

31 Barziza, Ultimus, R. Henderson Shuffler, editor. *The Adventures of A Prisoner of War.* Austin, Texas: University of Texas Press, 1964.

32 Gragg, Rod, editor. *The Illustrated Confederate Reader.* New York, New York: Harper and Row, Publishers, 1989.

33 Lenoir County Historical Association. *200 Years of Progress.* Kinston, North Carolina: Kinston-Lenoir County Bicentennial Commission, 1981.

34 Norton, Herman. *Rebel Religion.* St. Louis, Missouri: The Bethany Press, 1961.

35 Pitts, Charles F. *Chaplains in Gray–The Confederate Chaplains' Story.* Nashville, Tennessee: Broadman Press, 1957.

36 Gooding, Corporal James Henry, Company C, 54th Massachusetts Colored.

37 Jackman, John S. *Diary of a Confederate Soldier.* Columbia, South Carolina: University of South Carolina Press, 1990.

38 Wilkinson, Warren. *Mother, May You Never See the Sights I Have Seen.* New York, New York: Harper & Row Publishers, 1990.

39 Rhodes, Elisha Hunt. *All For the Union.* New York, New York: Orion Books, 1985.

40 Prichard, Robert. *A History of the Episcopal Church.* Harrisburg, Pennsylvania: Moorehouse Press, 1991.

41 Spencer, Bonnell. *Ye Are The Body.* West Park, New York: Holy Cross Publications, 1965.

42 Chitty, Arthur Benjamin, Jr. *Reconstruction at Sewanee.* Sewanee, Tennessee: The University Press, 1954.

43 Thomas, Albert Sidney. *A Historical Account of the Protestant Episcopal Church in South Carolina 1820-1957.* Columbia, South Carolina: R.L. Bryan Co., 1957.

44 Jones, Rev. J. William. *Christ in the Camp.* Atlanta, Georgia: The Martin & Hoyt Co., 1887.

45 Taylor, 1863, Minutes of the 1863 South Carolina Episcopal Diocesean Convention.

46 Walker, 1970, The 1844 Methodist Episcopal Church.

47 DuBose, William Porcher. *The Christian Ministry: A Sermon Preached at the Ordination of the Rev. O.T. Porcher, Abbeville, S.C., May 15, 1870.* Charleston, S.C.: n.p., 1870.

48 Booty, John E. *The Church in History.* New York, New York: Seabury Press, 1979.

49 Safford, James. *The Topography, Geology, and Water Supply of Sewanee, Tennessee.* Nashville, TN: A. B. Tavel, 1893

50 Fairbanks, George R. *History of The University of the South.* Jacksonville, Florida: The H & W.B. Drew Co., 1905.

51 DuBose, William Porcher. *The Soteriology of the New Testament.* New York, New York: MacMillan Company, 1892.

52 DuBose, William Porcher. *The Ecumenical Councils. Vol. III of Ten Epochs of Church History,* John Fulton, editor. New York, New York: The Christian Literature Company, 1896.

53 DuBose, William Porcher. *The Gospel in the Gospels.* New York, New York: Longman's, Green, and Co., 1906.

54 DuBose, William Porcher. *The Gospel According to St. Paul.* New York, New York: Longman's, Green, and Co., 1907.

55 DuBose, William Porcher. *High Priesthood and Sacrifice: An Exposition of the Epistle to the Hebrews,* The Bishop Paddock Lectures at the General Theological Seminary. New York, New York: Longman's, Green, and Co., 1908.

56 Thomas, John P. *Historical Sketch of the South Carolina Military Academy.* Charleston, South Carolina: Walker, Evans & Cogswell, 1879 (reprinted in 1893).

57 Armentrout, Donald S. *A DuBose Reader.* Sewanee, Tennessee: The University of the South, 1984.

58 Luker, Ralph. *A Southern Tradition in Theology and Social Criticism-1830-1930.* New York, New York: The Edwin Mellen Press, 1984.

59 Mozley, James K. *The Doctrine of the Atonement.* London, England: Gerald Duckworth and Co., 1915.

60 Sanday, William. *The Life of Christ in Recent Research.* Oxford University Press: London, England, 1907.

61 Pittenger, Norman. *Unity in the Faith.* Greenwich, Connecticut: Seabury Press, 1957.

62 Ahlstrom, Sidney E. *A Religious History of the American People.* New Haven, Connecticut: Yale University Press, 1972.

## WORKS CONSULTED

Alexander, Jon, editor. *William Porcher DuBose: Selected Writings.* New York, New York: Paulist Press, 1988.

Bond, Col. O. J. *The Story of The Citadel.* Richmond, Virginia: Garrett and Massie, 1989.

Boyd, Natalie Jenkins, and Osmun Latrobe Coward. *The South Carolinians.* New York, New York: Vantage Press, 1968.

Commager, Henry Steele, editor. *The Blue and the Gray: The Story of the Civil War as Told by Participants.* Indianapolis, Indiana: Bobbs-Merrill Company, Inc., 1950.

Foote, Shelby. *The Civil War–A Narrative. Fort Sumter to Perryville.* New York, New York: Random House, 1958.

Freeman, Douglas Southhall. *Lee's Lieutenants: A Study in Command.* New York, New York: Charles Scribner's Sons, 1944.

Harwell, Richard B. *The Confederate Reader.* New York, New York: Longmans, Green and Co, 1957.

Lawton, John S. *Conflict in Christianity: A Study of British and American Christology from 1889-1914.* New York, New York: MacMillan, 1947.

Marshall, John S. *The Word Was Made Flesh: The Theology of William Porcher DuBose.* Sewanee, Tennessee: Sewanee University Press, 1949.

MacDonald, John. *Great Battles of the Civil War.* New York, New York: Macmillan Publishing Company, 1988.

Moehring, Eugene P., and Arleen Keylin, editors. *The Civil War Extra: From the Pages of the Charleston Mercury and the New York Times.* New York, New York: Arno Press, 1975.

Murray, J.O.F. *DuBose as a Prophet of Unity.* A Series of Lectures Delivered at The University of the South. London, England: SPCK, 1924.

Newman, Ralph, and E.B. Long. *The Civil War, Vol II.* New York, New York: Grosset and Dunlap, Inc., 1956.

Palfrey, Francis Winfrey. *The Antietam and Fredericksburg.* New York, New York: The Blue and the Gray Press, Distributors, 18??.

Parish, Peter J. *The American Civil War.* New York, New York: Holmes & Meier Publishers, 1975.

Pearce, Hugo A., editor. *The Citadel Alumni Directory.* Charleston, South Carolina: Association of Citadel Men, 1960.

Porter, A. Toomer. *Led On! Step by Step.* New York, New York: G. P. Putnam's Sons, 1898.

Rodenbough, Theo F. et al, editors. *The Photographic History of the Civil War.* New York, New York: The Fairfax Press, 1983.

Shotwell, Randolph Abbott. *Three Years in Battle.* Raleigh, North Carolina: North Carolina Historical Commission, 1931.

Sifakis, Stewart. *Who was Who in the Civil War.* New York, New York: Facts on File, Inc., 1988.

Warner, Ezra J. *Generals in Gray: Lives of the Confederate Commanders.* Baton Rouge, Louisiana: Louisiana State University Press, 1959.

## ORDER FORM

**Postal Orders:**   Paint Rock Publishing
118 Dupont Smith Lane
Kingston, TN 37763
(423) 376-3892

**Please Send the Following Books:**
*(I understand that I may return any books for full refund—for any reason, no questions)*

*Oh, Yes, I Want To Go Home*   ($12.95) : _____

*The Final Furlough*   ($13.95): _____

*I Have Looked Death In The Face*   ($13.95) : _____

SUBTOTAL:   $ _____

**Sales Tax:**  Please add 8.25%
for books shipped to
TN addresses.   **Sales Tax:** $ _____

**Shipping:** Book Rate: $3.00 for
first book and .75 cents for
each extra book *(shipping may take 3 weeks)*
Air Mail: $4.00 per book.   **Shipping:** $ _____

TOTAL:   $ _____

## SHIP BOOKS TO:

_____

NAME

_____

ADDRESS

_____

CITY                                    STATE                    ZIP

**ORDER NOW——THANK YOU**